CULTURE SMART!
UKRAINE

Anna Shevchenko

·K·U·P·E·R·A·R·D· MAR 2013

ISBN 978 1 85733 663 4
This book is also available as an e-book: eISBN 978 1 85733 664 1

British Library Cataloguing in Publication Data
A CIP catalogue entry for this book is available from the British Library

First published in Great Britain 2005
by Kuperard, an imprint of Bravo Ltd
59 Hutton Grove, London N12 8DS
Tel: +44 (0) 20 8446 2440 Fax: +44 (0) 20 8446 2441
www.culturesmart.co.uk
Inquiries: sales@kuperard.co.uk

Distributed in the United States and Canada
by Random House Distribution Services
1745 Broadway, New York, NY 10019
Tel: +1 (212) 572-2844 Fax: +1 (212) 572-4961
Inquiries: csorders@randomhouse.com

Series Editor Geoffrey Chesler
Design Bobby Birchall

Printed in Malaysia

About the Author

ANNA SHEVCHENKO is a Ukrainian-born business development consultant and the managing director of 3CN, a British-based company specializing in cross-cultural risk management. She speaks seven languages, and has an M.Phil. degree from Cambridge University. Anna has worked with key government and industry decision makers in Britain, Europe, and the CIS. She is the author of numerous articles and two books on cross-cultural communication, as well as two novels set in Ukraine: *Bequest*, published in 2010, and *Tony's Game*, out in September 2012.

The Culture Smart! series is continuing to expand.
For further information and latest titles visit
www.culturesmart.co.uk

The publishers would like to thank **CultureSmart!**Consulting for its help in researching and developing the concept for this series.

CultureSmart!Consulting creates tailor-made seminars and consultancy programs to meet a wide range of corporate, public-sector, and individual needs. Whether delivering courses on multicultural team building in the USA, preparing Chinese engineers for a posting in Europe, training call-center staff in India, or raising the awareness of police forces to the needs of diverse ethnic communities, it provides essential, practical, and powerful skills worldwide to an increasingly international workforce.

For details, visit www.culturesmartconsulting.com

CultureSmart!Consulting and **CultureSmart!** guides have both contributed to and featured regularly in the weekly travel program "Fast Track" on BBC World TV.

contents

contents

Map of Ukraine

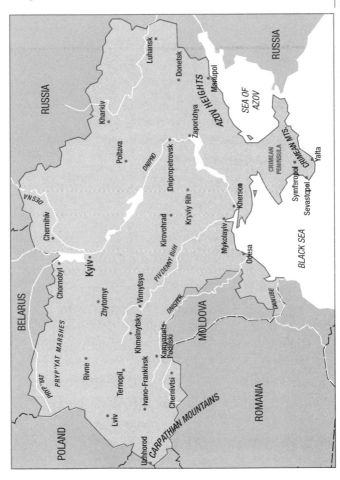

introduction

When you travel to Ukraine, you enter a country full of paradoxes. The Ukrainians are proud of their roots, and reticent about their recent past; the country participates in international space programs and produces the world's largest aircraft, but still lives in a world of superstitions. The Ukrainian way of life is a mix of the old Soviet legacy, centuries-old customs, and a search for a new European identity.

The word *ukraina* means "borderland," and indeed for centuries the country was a border province of great empires. Different states fought bloody wars for the fertile Ukrainian lands and tore the country to pieces. Its history has been a constant struggle for independence and freedom, and foreign domination has left indelible traces in the Ukrainian mentality: Ukrainians are fatalistic, patient, and resilient, and one of the most popular sayings translates as "Things will improve somehow."

The independent state of Ukraine is twenty years old, and in these two decades it has had its fair share of turmoil. The first years of independence saw the euphoria of freedom replaced by rampant inflation, poverty, and crime. Corruption became widespread, and frequently changing governments led to political uncertainty. Ukrainians lost count of elections, and the Orange Revolution, the great peaceful display of "people power" that overturned the results of rigged elections in 2004, turned sour. The country that lies on the crossroads of the famous historical trade routes—"from Varangians to Greeks" (north–south) and from Europe to Asia (east–west)—is now at the crossroads of its own destiny.

Marcel Proust once said, "The true voyage of discovery lies not in seeking new landscapes, but in having new eyes." We hope that *Culture Smart! Ukraine* will help you to come to the country with your eyes open. It will inform you about the historical, political, and religious background that continues to shape the Ukrainian psyche today. Using illustrative anecdotes, it describes present-day values and attitudes, and offers practical advice on what to expect and how to behave in different social circumstances. It aims to make you feel at ease, whether you are sitting at a generously spread Ukrainian dinner table, shopping in a market, or attending a formal business meeting.

Vitayemo!—Welcome to Ukraine!

Key Facts

Official Name	Ukraine (*Ukrayina*)	
Capital City	Kyiv	Pop. 2.64 million
Major Cities	Donetsk, Dnipropetrovsk, Kharkiv, Lviv, Odesa	
Area	233,090 sq. miles (603,700 sq. km)	The second-largest country in Europe, after Russia
Borders	Russia, Belarus, Poland, Slovakia, Hungary, Romania, and Moldova	
Climate	Moderate, with January av. temps. 19°F (-7°C) in the northeast and 39°F (+ 4°C) in the Crimean Peninsula	July av. temps. 66–70°F (19–21°C)
Currency	Hryvna (abbreviated to UAH)	1 hryvna = 100 kopiyky (plural) (the singular is kopiyka)
Population	45.8 million	The fifth-largest in Europe
Ethnic Makeup	78 percent Ukrainian. Russians are the largest minority (17 percent).	Also, Jews, Poles, Moldovans, Bulgarians, and Tatars
Language	Ukrainian	Russian is widely spoken and understood.
Religion	Mainly Orthodox. Ukrainian Orthodox Church (Moscow Patriarchate and Kyivan Patriarchate); Ukrainian Autocephalous Orthodox Church	Other religions: Catholic (Ukrainian Greek Catholic Church and Roman Catholic Church), Judaism, Islam

Government	The president is head of state. The Verkhovna Rada (parliament) of Ukraine has legislative power, while the cabinet of ministers is the main body of executive power.	There are twenty-four administrative regions (*oblasts*), the Autonomous Republic of Crimea, and two cities of Republican Authorization (Kyiv and Sevastopol).
Media	*Zerkalo Nedeli* (political weekly, English-language pages), *Den* (daily, English-language pages), *Kyiv Post* (English-language daily), *Ukrayinska Pravda* (online news, English-language pages) News agencies: Interfax (Ukraine), UNIAN, Ukrinform	
Electricity	220 volts, 50 Hz and a standard two-prong plug	Adaptors are needed for US and UK appliances.
Radiation	Levels are constantly monitored, are minimal, and are not a threat to health.	
Video/TV	PAL/SECAM system	International satellite TV channels available at four- and five-star hotels
Internet Domain	.ua	
Telephone	The international dialing code for Ukraine is +38. The code for Kyiv is 044.	To call out of Ukraine, dial 8 (for outside the city), then 10, followed by the country code.
Time Zone	GMT + 2 hours	In summer clocks go forward by one hour.

chapter one

LAND & PEOPLE

GEOGRAPHICAL SNAPSHOT

When you travel through the picturesque region of Transcarpathia in the Western Ukraine, admiring its flower-filled valleys and fast rivers, you might spot a small monument near the Slovak border. And, if you studied Latin, you will be able to translate the inscription, marked by the Vienna Geographical Society in 1911, as " . . . with a scale of meridians and parallels, the center of Europe has been established here."

So, what is this country in the geographical center of Europe like? Bordered by Russia in the east and northeast, Belarus in the north, Poland, Slovakia, and Hungary in the west, and Romania and Moldova in the southwest, it is the second-largest European country in territory after Russia, with the fifth-largest population (approx. 45.8 million); 78 percent of the population are ethnic Ukrainians, 17 percent of the population are Russian, with other ethnic minorities, mainly from the bordering countries, making up the remaining 5 percent. The Crimean Tatars, who were forcibly deported to

Central Asia in 1944, have been allowed to settle in Crimea. So far, around 250,000 have returned.

Administratively, Ukraine consists of twenty-four *oblasts* (regions) and one Autonomous Republic (Crimea). The capital, Kyiv (formerly "Kiev"), has a population of 2.64 million.

The Carpathian Mountains and alpine meadows (*polonyny*) in the west descend to the rolling hills of Podillya, and to the thick forest of Polissya further east. The steppes stretch all the way south, to the coasts of the Black Sea and the Sea of Azov, where the Crimean Peninsula enjoys a Mediterranean climate.

Flying over Ukraine in summer, you will see endless golden fields—"the breadbasket of Europe" lives up to its name. Even the blue and yellow Ukrainian flag reflects two of the country's treasures: clear skies and wheat fields. The temperate continental climate and a quarter of

the world's rich black soil, *chornozem*, made the land ideal for agriculture. As Ukrainians say, "Even if you plant a spade, it will grow in Ukrainian soil." And, although only 33 percent of the population live in the rural areas, the Ukrainians (including those who live in the cities) are known for their "farmer's" mentality. They are self-reliant, hardworking, and individualistic, and they are ready to face hardships and laugh at themselves.

The longest river, the Dnipro (Dnieper), flows through the center of the country, and serves as a natural division between east and west. This divide is not only geographical.

The East–West Divide
The three biggest Ukrainian industrial cities—Kharkiv, city of engineers, metallurgical Dnipropetrovsk, and mining Donetsk—with their giant post-Soviet industrial plants, are situated in the eastern part of Ukraine. Western Ukraine is

more rural and traditional. Apart from economic development, there is a national aspect. As large areas of Western Ukraine were parts of Hungary, Czechoslovakia, and Poland until the end of the Second World War, Western Ukraine is much more pro-European, and sees Ukraine's future in the new Europe. Eastern Ukraine supports closer economic ties with Russia—not surprisingly, as most of the eight million ethnic Russians live here.

On August 24, 1991, the Ukrainian Parliament declared Ukraine's independence. On December 1, 1991, in a nationwide referendum, over 90 percent of the voters confirmed the Act of Independence. Ukraine, a former republic of the Soviet Union, became a state in its own right. To understand what this meant for Ukraine at the threshold of the twenty-first century, it is essential to look at the country's history.

A BRIEF HISTORY

It is often said that Ukraine is enriched by nature but robbed by history. For centuries, neighboring states fought bloody wars to control its fertile lands. Foreign domination has left indelible traces in the Ukrainian mentality: Ukrainians are fatalistic, patient, and resilient, and, as we've seen, one of their most popular sayings translates as "Things will improve somehow."

Kyivan Rus

The Ukrainians trace their ancestry to the early eastern Slavic tribes. According to legend, three brothers—Kiy, Shchek, and Khoryv, from the Slavic Polian tribe—founded the settlement of Kyiv in the sixth century CE. They called it Kyiv after the eldest brother. In 882 CE the Scandinavian prince Oleg

captured Kyiv, killed the local Polian rulers Ascold and Dir, and proclaimed, "Here will be the mother of Rus cities." The Rus were the dominant Viking clan. Kyiv became an important point on the Viking trade route—called "From Varangians [Vikings] to Greeks"—from the Baltic to the Mediterranean. In the tenth century Kyiv was the capital of Kyivan Rus, a powerful empire extending from the Baltic Sea in the north to the Black Sea in the south.

In 988 Prince Vladimir introduced Orthodox Christianity to Rus, albeit in a peculiar way. He announced to the Byzantine emperors Constantine and Basil his decision to be christened, and took his fleet to Crimea, to the Byzantine city of Khersones, for the purpose. He returned to Kyiv and ordered the pagan wooden idols to be cast down and floated down the River Dnipro. While his subjects watched in horror, Vladimir appeared on the hill with the council of Greek priests. At his signal, all the people there, adults and children, were  commanded to step into the freezing waters of the Dnipro to be baptized.

Kyivan Rus flourished during the rule of Yaroslav, Vladimir's son. Known as Yaroslav the Wise, he created the first legal code, "the Russian truth," carried out grand construction projects, and avoided wars by marrying his daughters to European monarchs. His eldest daughter, Anna, became the first literate queen of France when she married Henry I in Reims Cathedral in 1051. On being consecrated as Queen, she took her oath placing her hand on the Gospel that she had brought from Kyiv.

The prosperity of Kyivan Rus attracted invaders from the southern steppes. The city of Kyiv and the power of Kyivan Rus were destroyed by the Mongol Baty Khan's conquest in 1240. The siege of Kyiv lasted several weeks. The Mongol army was so enormous that, according to the chronicler, "You could not hear anything for the creak of their carts, the roar of their camels . . . The land of Rus was filled with enemy." The city was burned down, and thousands were killed. The lands of Kyivan Rus were divided by the principalities of Galicia, Volynia, and Muscovy—later Poland, Lithuania, and Russia.

In the fifteenth century the Lithuanian prince Alexander granted the city of Kyiv a certain degree of independence under the Magdeburg Right, the European code of municipal self-government, in accordance with which the citizens of Kyiv were governed by the members of an elected self-government and a court. The Magdeburg Right was effective in Kyiv until 1834.

The Cossack State

Cossacks are one of the Ukrainian symbols of national independence. Their mystique lives on in Ukrainian proverbs, legends, and songs. Rebels and warriors, protectors of the borders, freedom fighters, adventurers—who were they in reality?

The word "Cossack" comes from the Turkish word meaning "free man." More than five centuries ago the mass escape of Ukrainian serfs from feudal oppression gave birth to the Cossack movement. These runaway serfs settled along the empty southern steppes, at the delta of the Dnipro River. In order to protect their settlements from the devastating raids of the Crimean Tatars, they developed various forms of self-defense. In these circumstances, Cossack soldiers had to be brave and agile, ready to fight in the steppes and at sea, and strong in their faith and in action. For more than two hundred years they resisted Turks, Tatars, and Polish domination.

In the middle of the sixteenth century, the Cossacks formed their own state—Zaporizhska Sych—and created their own democratic military administrative system. They had their own legal proceedings and military councils. The governing body was the Army Kysch, headed by hetmans, or Cossack chieftains. The world's first constitution was written for the Cossack state by the hetman Philip Orlyk in 1710.

The Cossacks' horsemanship, powers of endurance, ability to withstand pain, and ability to drink were legendary. The typical Cossack had a long moustache, a shaven head with a single lock of hair, and an earring. When a former Ukrainian Minister of Defense was asked why the Ukrainian army did not adopt Cossacks as examples of bravery, his reply was: "I didn't like the uniform and the drinking habits."

The Cossack hetman Bogdan Khmelnitsky played a fateful role in the history of Ukraine. He led the Ukrainian uprising against Polish expansionism, and in 1654 signed the Pereyaslav Agreement with Russia to provide mutual defense against the Poles. Many Ukrainians consider this a tragic point in their history, as Moscow turned this agreement of mutual military and political assistance into an act of union— incorporating Ukraine into the Russian empire. The modern benefit of that agreement, as Ukrainians often ironically point out, is the fact that in 1954 the Soviet leader Nikita Khrushchev ceded the Crimean Peninsula, with its Mediterranean climate, spas, and seaside resorts, to Ukraine as a gift to mark the three-hundredth anniversary of Khmelnitsky's union with Russia.

Another hetman, Ivan Mazepa, made a desperate attempt to save the country, and signed an agreement with Charles XII of Sweden to fight against the Russian Tsar, Peter the Great. However, Swedish troops suffered a disastrous defeat at the battle of Poltava in 1709. Russia continued the aggressive acquisition of Cossack lands, gradually abolishing the privileges of the Ukrainian Cossacks. Ukraine was called "*Malorossiya*"—"Little Russia"—and became a powerless province of the Russian empire.

By 1775, by order of the Russian Empress Catherine the Great, Zaporizhska Sych was completely destroyed, both as a legal entity and physically, and the Ukrainian lands were divided between Russia and Austria.

In Ukraine you will see the Cossack heritage everywhere—in monuments, paintings, names of streets and restaurants, even in the names of brands of vodka. Their dance troupes are legendary. A popular Ukrainian vodka (*horilka*) is called "Hetman," and has portraits and brief

biographies of Cossack chieftains on the labels.

The Nineteenth-Century Independence Movement
Though Ukrainian sovereignty was crushed, prominent intellectuals never abandoned hope of reinstating independence. The national Ukrainian spirit found its outlet in both secret and legal organizations, such as the Brotherhood of Cyril and Methodius, whose members included Taras Grygorovich Shevchenko (1814–61)—a poet, artist, and symbol of the revival of national culture, language, and consciousness. "There is something appealing about a nation whose greatest hero is a poet and a painter," comments the writer Linda Hodges. Shevchenko's book of poetry, *Kobzar*, was kept in every home next to the Bible, and his poem "Testament" was known and repeated as a prayer. His words, "Fight and you shall win," were quoted in Ukrainian by the former US president Bill Clinton during his visit to Ukraine.

There are numerous monuments to Taras Shevchenko, not only in Ukraine, but also in Moscow, Toronto, Washington, and other cities

across the world. A black taxi driver in Washington, when asked whether he knew whom the monument honored, replied, "I don't know his name, but I know he was a good man. A poet, who fought against slavery." And indeed Shevchenko, a serf himself, whose freedom was bought in 1838 by a Russian painter, spent his life writing about serfdom, the suppression of Ukrainian culture by Russia, and Russian autocracy. His poem "The Heretic" (1845) spoke of his dream of a free brotherhood of all Slavs. He became a professor at Kyiv in 1845, and founded an organization for radical social reform.

Shevchenko was severely punished for his views: he was sent to a Siberian labor battalion for ten years, and was never allowed to live in Ukraine again. He died in St. Petersburg at the age of forty-seven. But the seeds he planted in his poems grew, and the Ukrainian national independence movement became so widespread that in 1865 the Tsarist government banned the use of the Ukrainian language in public. Ukrainian culture was, again, suppressed.

The Tragic Twentieth Century

During the twentieth century Ukraine lost almost a third of its population—around fifteen million people—as a result of the artificial famine, the Second World War, and mass repressions. The memories of this recent past are an integral part of the Ukrainian view of life, though it is only recently that people have been finding the voice and the courage to talk about them. They define the Ukrainian mentality and have their reflection in the language, in key words such as "to bring up" (*vyhovaty*), which comes from the word *hovaty* meaning "to hide"—to hide and protect the child from wars and enemies.

Changing Hands

Following the First World War and the collapse of the Russian Tsarist authority, Ukraine had a chance to gain independence, but in the chaos of the civil war none of the factions could win decisive support. In the years 1917–20 Kyiv, according to different estimates, changed hands between fourteen and eighteen times. There was fighting between Ukrainian leaders of different orientations, pro-Moscow Bolsheviks, Tsarist White Guards, Polish, and German occupants. Western Ukraine has also changed hands so many times that there is a popular joke about an old man in a village in Transcarpathia. When asked about his life, he said, "I was born in Austro-Hungary, went to school in Czechoslovakia, served in the Hungarian army and then went to prison in the Soviet Union. Now I live in independent Ukraine!" "Oh, you must have traveled and seen a lot!" "Oh, no, I have never left my village!"

On January 22, 1918, the Ukrainian government, Tsentralna Rada, proclaimed Ukrainian independence. Briefly, during 1919–21, Eastern and Western Ukraine united to form an independent Ukrainian government that was ultimately crushed by Russian Bolsheviks. Western Ukraine fell under the control of Poland; the rest officially became part of the USSR in 1922. For those twenty-three million Ukrainians in the eastern part of Ukraine, life under Soviet rule was overwhelmed by tragedy.

Holodomor—The Great Famine

Vyacheslav Lypinsky, the Ukrainian historian and sociologist, noted that, "love for one's land is the primary dynamic force of the Ukrainian." The inclination of Ukrainians toward private land ownership has been traditional since Cossack times, when the runaway serfs got the chance of owning the land they worked on.

As a result, Stalin's policy ofcollectivization— taking away the land from independent farmers and creating collective farms under complete Communist control—moved much more slowly in Ukraine than in Russia. Once, talking to Winston Churchill, Stalin referred to collectivization as a terrible struggle that had lasted four years and involved ten million people. Most of these people were defenseless Ukrainian peasants. Grain, the source of Ukrainian pride and livelihood, became Stalin's weapon in his drive to press the Ukrainian peasants into submission, force them into the collectives, and ensure a steady supply of grain for Soviet industrialization.

In 1932 the Communist Party adopted a new plan for grain-collection quotas in Ukraine, which were increased by 44 percent. This was unachievable, and the result was a massive shortage of food. Roadblocks were set up to stop Ukrainians from moving out of their region, and any attempts to grind grain or collect crops from the vegetable gardens were regarded as a crime against the state and punished by execution by firing squad.

While a hundred million tons of grain were taken out of Ukraine, the starving peasants were consigned to a slow death. The highest death rates were in the grain-growing provinces of Poltava, Dnipropetrovsk, Kirovohrad, and Odesa, where

20–25 percent of the population died; in many individual villages the death rates were higher.

The Great Famine of 1932–33 took an estimated seven million lives in fifteen months. People died at a rate of seventeen every minute: 25,000 every day. One-third of those who died of starvation were children.

The Russian poet Boris Pasternak, author of the Nobel Prize-winning novel *Doctor Zhivago*, wrote, "In the early 1930s, there was a movement among writers to travel to the collective farms and gather material about the new life of the village. I wanted to be with everyone else and likewise made a trip with the aim of writing a book. What I saw could not be expressed in words. There was such inhuman, unimaginable misery, such a terrible disaster, that it began to seem almost abstract, it would not fit within the bounds of consciousness. I fell ill. For an entire year I could not write."

The Great Famine was a forbidden topic in the Soviet era, and remained a secret tragedy of the buried nation. Only in 1998 did the President of Ukraine officially recognize the famine by proclaiming an annual National Day of Remembrance of the Famine Victims on the fourth Saturday of November. On November 28, 2006, Ukraine's parliament, the Verkhovna Rada, passed a law recognizing the 1932–33 *Holodomor* as an act of genocide against the Ukrainian people.

The famine was followed by the years of the notorious Stalin purges. From 1937 thousands of people disappeared overnight without explanation, executed for "nationalism and espionage." In 1938 all 115 members of the Soviet Ukrainian government were executed. By 1941 the NKVD, the Soviet secret police, had arrested nineteen million Soviets; seven million were shot or died in the Siberian camps; at least a million of these were Ukrainians.

The Second World War
During the Second World War, under the Nazi occupation, Ukraine suffered the highest population loss in Europe. Over eight million Ukrainians perished during the war, including 1.5 million Jews. The worst atrocity occurred at Baby Yar, a large ravine on the northern edge of Kyiv. In just two days, September 29 and 30, 1941, almost 34,000 Jews were murdered by German SS killing squads, and a further 70,000 bodies were added to the mass grave in 1941–3. Baby Yar became the symbol of the Jewish Holocaust in Ukraine.

Ukrainian cities and villages bore the brunt first of the Nazis' advance to Stalingrad and then of the Soviet Army counteroffensive. In 1943 the Ukrainian film director Alexandr Dovzhenko wrote, "The fate of humankind is decided in Ukrainian fields and villages, in fire and flame, on our misfortune. So ill-fated is our land. So miserable is our lot." More than a million Ukrainians were taken to Germany to work as *Ostarbeiters* and then, too scared to come back to Stalin's regime, were displaced after the war, scattered around the world.

It is true that a number of Ukrainians served as guards in the concentration camps of Treblinka, Sobibor, and Belzec, and around 30,000 Ukrainians, mainly from Western Ukraine, fought against the Soviet Army in a special German 14th division, Halychyna. But for every story of collaboration there are several examples of the Ukrainians' heroic struggle against the Nazi regime, joining partisan groups and Soviet Army units, and saving Jews from the Holocaust.

The Postwar Years
Resistance against the Soviet Union continued in Ukraine until as late as the 1950s. In all, half a million Ukrainians were deported to the Gulag prison and labor camps in the 1950s. Russians were brought in to occupy all key positions in the

government. Stalin's death in 1953 brought a
political " thaw," and the 1960s saw an upsurge
of culture, particularly of poetry and art. However,
the authorities were increasingly alarmed by
cultural figures such as historians and writers who
led protests against the longstanding Russification
of Ukraine. In 1965, and later during the "general
pogrom" of 1972, thousands were imprisoned in
labor camps for "anti-Soviet agitation," or sent for
indefinite periods to psychiatric hospitals. Vasyl
Stus, for example, a Ukrainian dissident poet,
was killed in a Soviet labor camp. Some prisoners
were released as late as 1987. The Jews were given
permission to leave, and more than 300,000 Jews
have emigrated to the West in recent years.

Chornobyl

The Chornobyl disaster became a symbol of the
decay of the Soviet system. On April 26, 1986,
Reactor N 4 at the Chornobyl nuclear
plant near Kyiv suffered a runaway
chain reaction, causing the worst
nuclear accident in history.

The official figures state that there
were 10,000 deaths as a direct result of
the accident, but the shadow of Chornobyl
remains over Ukraine. More than three and a half
million Ukrainians were affected, one million of
them children. Thousands upon thousands were

evacuated from their homes, often with a couple of hours' notice, and never to return, as their possessions were contaminated. The famous Ukrainian poet Lina Kostenko wrote that "a radiation meter was no good for measuring the devastation of the soul." The Chornobyl plant was finally shut down in 2000.

Paradoxically, the Chornobyl tragedy became the catalyst for the declaration of independence. It exposed the shocking, blatant lies and secretive behavior of the Soviet officials, who were overwhelmingly denying the scale of the accident. Widespread discontent across the nation gave a boost to the opposition movement. In 1990 the Ukrainian People's Movement for Restructuring, Rukh, founded in Kyiv, won parliamentary seats across the country.

On August 19 there was an attempted coup when conservative Soviet leaders tried to restore central Communist Party control over the USSR.

 In response, in a special session on August 24, the parliament of the Ukrainian SSR overwhelmingly approved the Act of Declaration of Independence of Ukraine. It also called for a national referendum on support for the Declaration. In December 1991 Ukraine voted overwhelmingly for independence.

Although since independence the cloud of Soviet fear has been slowly lifting, the older generation is still reluctant to talk openly about the totalitarian regime, about the way they lived. When in Ukraine, don't be surprised by heated discussions in the press and at dinner tables about certain events in Ukrainian history. It remains a contested history, seen from different viewpoints, depending on the speaker's age, location, education, and experience. Ukrainian people are rediscovering their nation's past. The search for the truth continues.

GOVERNMENT AND POLITICS

When Ukraine proclaimed its independence on August 24, 1991, it moved from being a "member of the family of Soviet nations" to a sovereign state. Ukrainian statehood had to be created in a short period of  time against the backdrop of severe economic crisis, a kaleidoscope of governments, and the social and financial consequences of the Chornobyl nuclear disaster.

Building a new political system was not an easy undertaking in itself, but consensus is not the strongest feature of the Ukrainian mentality. "There are always five hetmans for three Cossacks" (meaning that there are always more people to make decisions than to execute them), says a Ukrainian proverb. Reflecting this inability to reach consensus, the new Ukrainian political system has undergone many changes since the Orange Revolution of 2004.

In 2004 the results of the presidential election split the country. Claiming that the vote had been rigged, thousands of orange-clad protesters poured onto the streets of Kyiv in freezing temperatures to support the defeated pro-Western candidate, the former central banker Viktor Yushenko. After ten days of demonstrations and picketing of government buildings, the Supreme Court eventually declared the results invalid and ordered a rerun. Yushenko duly defeated his rival, the Russian-backed Viktor Yanukovych, by a very narrow margin, and in January 2005 became the third president of independent Ukraine.

The country's political forces find it difficult to reach an agreement. Government decisions have been characterized as "hot air"—on one occasion literally: in February 2008 protesting members of the parliament, the Verkhovna Rada, staged a walk-out, leaving inflated balloons on their seats.

The Ukrainian political scene has often been compared to that of Italy: governments come and go, but the business of state carries on regardless.

RELATIONS WITH RUSSIA

The first thing a Ukrainian will say to you is, "We are not Russians." True Ukrainian identity, though suppressed for years, has survived through centuries of wars, colonization, and political repression. Before 1991 Ukraine did not exist, in many Western minds, as a country. In fact, one of the leading British charities, organizing assistance for Chornobyl victims, referred to Ukraine as "a region in southern Russia."

Ukrainians and Russians share the same historic roots: Kyivan Rus was the cradle of three eastern Slavic nations: Russian, Byelorussian, and Ukrainian. There are three centuries of joint history, when Ukraine was a part of Tsarist Russia and then the Soviet empire, and a common Orthodox religion. After centuries of Russification everybody in Ukraine speaks and understands Russian.

And yet it is impossible to see these two nations as identical. The languages are distinctly different, as is the mentality. Apart from the Orthodox Church of Moscow Patriarchate and the Orthodox Church of Kyiv Patriarchate, Ukraine has a significant number of Greek and Roman Catholics (mainly in the west), as well as many traditions and customs deeply rooted in pagan beliefs.

Russia has had the historic experience of being the ruling nation at the center of an enormous empire. Ukraine, however, became an outer province of this empire, and even in name was reduced to "*Malorossiya*"—"Little Russia."

At the beginning of the 1920s, when a sovereign Ukrainian state was proclaimed, Leon Trotsky, head of the Revolutionary Military Soviet of the Russian Federation, wrote, " . . . we must get Ukraine into Russia's fold. Without Ukraine no Russia is possible. Without Ukrainian coal, iron, ores, and bread, without the Black Sea, Russia cannot exist—it will suffocate." No wonder that in 1922 the Russian Bolsheviks turned to aggression.

Russia still regards Ukraine as a sphere of vital national interest. Russians often patronizingly

refer to Ukrainians as "our Slavic brothers,"
while Ukrainians have always exercised a cautious
respect toward an "elder brother"—Russia. In fact,
Russia has become more of an ever-watching
"Big Brother." "Russian democracy ends where
the Ukrainian question begins," wrote Volodymyr
Vernadsky, a Ukrainian academician.

Whatever political differences there may be,
however, the two countries have very close social
and economic ties. Eight million Russians in the
Ukrainian industrial east and Crimea speak
Russian as their first language. The Russian Black
Sea Fleet has its base in the Crimean city of
Sevastopol. Russia is Ukraine's largest trading
partner. It supplies more than a third of Ukraine's
energy needs, and Russian oil and gas flow
through Ukrainian pipelines to Europe. Ukraine
recognizes Russia as its key strategic partner and
wants to build relations with it on the principles
of equal partnership, as a good neighbor.

chapter two

VALUES &
ATTITUDES

THE UKRAINIAN CHARACTER

Stereotypes are often called "mental cookie cutters"—they force a simple pattern upon a complex cultural world, and place all members of society into a specific category. In the 1920s the social psychologist Walter Lippman defined the stereotype as "the picture of the world that a person has in his head." The way you perceive other people is often a reflection of how you see the world and your place in it.

A Canadian professor once asked a group of students who had just spent three months in Kyiv to list the qualities that define the Ukrainian character. Half the students were asked to note down the positive qualities, the other half the negative ones. They came up with unexpected results. The positive qualities included such characteristics as "hardworking, emotional, and direct," while the negative list had "greedy, moody, and rude." According to the "picture in one's head" the same person was seen as a "hardworking, good earner" by one student and as "greedy" by another.

It is also important to understand that the Ukrainians' " picture of the world" varies from the generation that studied and lived under the Soviet regime to the students who grew up in the new Ukrainian state. Older people still crave the "good old days" and the stability of the regimented regime, while the young welcome independence and the freedom brought by democracy. Attitudes to religion, gender, and money have changed dramatically in the last twenty years. This chapter will attempt to describe what it means to think and act as a Ukrainian.

The imaginary world of folk songs and fairy tales is a succinct expression of the values, attitudes, and beliefs of any nation. A popular Ukrainian tale, "Rukavychka" ("The Mitten"), tells the story of a mouse who finds a lost mitten in a frozen winter wood, and decides to make it a home. Other animals, from a frog to a wolf, in turn find the mitten, and the mouse welcomes them all. The mitten stretches to provide shelter, warmth, and protection for everyone. This tale reflects two basic Ukrainian values: hospitality and community spirit.

HOSPITALITY

Ukrainian hospitality extends beyond the limits of time and economy. Even in the hardest times, when the shops were empty and the food lines were long, the spirit of hospitality remained. The best food is always for the guest, as is the best room and the best bed linen. Ukrainians will always give up their free time to entertain guests and show them around. Some visitors might find such attention overwhelming.

Too Kind?

A British student was staying with a Ukrainian family. After a week her hosts found her in tears. She said to the shocked family that she felt like a captive, as she had no time to herself, and no chance to go out to explore the country on her own. There always was a family friend or a relative there, volunteering to take her out, and every ten minutes she was asked whether she was hungry, tired, or cold. She found it difficult to cope with the pressure of Ukrainian hospitality.

COMMUNITY SPIRIT

Ukrainian society has always been based on close ties, and the "Rukavychka" story above illustrates it well. Community spirit is evident in times of hardship, sadness, and joy. It became a survival mechanism to enable the nation to get through its tragic history. When parents were killed in the war, or died of starvation, godparents, friends, and neighbors would take care of the children.

A funeral is often organized with the help of friends and neighbors, easing the burden on the grieving relatives. Where foreigners might see this as interference, Ukrainians feel a desire to rally round. In the Ukrainian tradition, the relatives and friends get together on the ninth and the fortieth days after the funeral, as it is believed that the soul stays on earth for forty days, traveling around to say last farewells. These gatherings play an important role in supporting the family.

Ukrainian villages still keep the tradition of helping each other with the harvest, such as when neighbors, friends, and relatives all come over for a "potato digging party." With everybody setting to work the job is soon finished—then the tables are laid and the party begins!

The constraints of Soviet accommodation also enhanced the community spirit. There are still traces of Soviet invention, such as the "communal apartment," in which up to ten families along one corridor shared a kitchen and bathroom. One had no option but to get along with one's neighbors! Recent articles in the Ukrainian press felt the need to explain the notion of "private space."

FAMILY LOYALTY

Over 70 percent of Ukrainians live in small apartments with two or three bedrooms, often with three generations under one roof. However, the housing shortage is only one reason for this close-knit family pattern. An extended family is a source of help and support, and there is a strong tradition of duty toward and respect for the elderly. At the time of the collapse of the Soviet system, when most retired people lost their life savings, those who had children, or even nephews and nieces, survived as a result of financial support from them. And, of course, they help to look after the grandchildren.

Parents protect—sometimes overprotect—their children. There is a joke, "Let me help my children until they retire, and then the state will look after them," and there is some truth in it. The Western idea of "leaving the nest" is replaced in Ukraine by the notion of the lifelong bond with parents. A family law, adopted in Ukraine in 2004, has brought in penalties for adult children not supporting ailing parents. Ukrainians would trust their own siblings and relatives before anybody else, and one result of this is that many recently established private firms are family enterprises.

However, the idea of the extended family safety net has been changing along with social and geographical factors. Previously, many young couples married at the age of eighteen or twenty and lived with their parents; now the tendency is to gain some independence first. Family dynamics is changing, too. The number of marriages in Ukraine fell by 30 percent in 2007–10 compared to 1987–90, more families are separated because the breadwinner is earning money abroad, and more women choose to have children later in life and out of wedlock.

WOMEN IN SOCIETY

Throughout Ukrainian history, with its centuries of trials and wars, men were away fighting for their country and strong, independent-minded women raised children and farmed the land. In contrast to Western Europe, in Ukraine in the sixteenth and seventeenth centuries it was the material status of women, not the social status of their husbands, that determined their position in society. Women in the cities could become local governors and take an active part in politics.

The idea of a Ukrainian woman-mother is reflected in the folklore; Ukraine itself is often called "Mother Ukraine." In the south, in the steppes near the Azov Sea, you can still find pagan statues, or stone *babas*—life-size female figures erected by nomads between the eleventh and thirteenth centuries. They were worshiped up to the nineteenth century as symbols of the protectress, the goddess of fertility, the mother of all living things.

For Ukrainian women the sense of duty toward family and children has always been of prime importance. The negative side of this is that a woman in Ukraine is often seen primarily as a "hearthkeeper" and a maintainer of family traditions rather than as an individual in her own right. As a consequence, many women suffer from abuse at home for the sake of the children. A law to prevent violence in the family was passed by Parliament only in 2001, ten years after Ukraine had gained independence.

Although the Ukrainian word for "to marry" (*odrujitysya*) can be translated as "to get a friend," society still sees a woman in her traditional role. This joke sums up the feelings of the Ukrainian man: "My wife deals with the minor problems in the family—what to eat, where to go, how to bring up the children—while I deal with the global issues—such as whether there is life on Mars."

In Soviet times, the role of "worker" was added to that of a mother, as 95 percent of Soviet families could not survive on one income. Many women became cogs in the Soviet production wheels, often doing harder, lower-paid work.

However, those who expect to see Ukrainian women of indefinite age wearing drab gray clothes and scarves will be pleasantly surprised. Women in Ukraine are referred to as "the weaker, but more beautiful" part of the nation. They are proud of their femininity and spend a lot of time and money on clothes and careful grooming. A leading Ukrainian businesswoman said in a TV interview that she would definitely cancel an important meeting if her hands were not beautifully manicured. Another woman, an MP, wears figure-hugging designer dresses to parliamentary meetings, as she feels that "the secret weapon of femininity helps me to fight gender inequality."

Ukrainian women are used to compliments and flirting. Chivalry is still an important part of male behavior. Men are expected to assist women with coats, carry heavy bags, and help them in and out of cars and buses. At city crossroads you often see huge billboards showing photographs of smiling girls and inscriptions, such as "Happy Birthday Natalia! [or Iryna, or Tetyana . . .]"—extravagant declarations of love, from those who can afford it, to their sweethearts.

Although Ukrainian society is still dominated by men, there is a Ukrainian proverb that says "The man is a head, but the woman is a neck. The man looks where the neck turns."

ATTITUDES TOWARD ETHNIC MINORITIES

With its crossroads position and borders with seven countries, it is not surprising that ethnic minorities constitute about 22 percent of the Ukrainian population. The Ukrainian Law on Ethnic Minorities (1992) has been accepted by the Council of Europe as one of the best in Eastern and Central Europe. Nevertheless, ethnic minorities do not hold an equal place in society. Police fail to investigate complaints about skinhead racist attacks; there have been vandalism of synagogues and anti-Semitic expressions in the media. Covert racism is a problem, with police subjecting people with a dark skin to arbitrary detentions.

Ukraine is often referred to as a "transit country." Problems stem from the numbers of incoming refugees, particularly from the Caucasus and Southeast Asia. In 2001 a law was passed that gives refugees the same rights to medical care, education, employment, and choice of residence as Ukrainian nationals.

The Jewish Population

Before the 1990s the Jewish community in Ukraine was the fourth-largest in the world, after the USA, Israel, and Russia. Ukraine was home to a Jewish population for over a thousand years, but in Tsarist Russia anti-Semitism, based on religious hostility and economic resentment, was rampant. It led to a wave of pogroms in Ukraine at the end of the nineteenth century and during the civil war of 1918–21. After the collapse of the Soviet Union, efforts were made to revive the Jewish community, and today there are seventeen synagogues and twenty-two Jewish day schools.

Ukraine had been a stronghold of Hassidism, Orthodox Judaism's mass mystical and revivalist movement. Every year the small town of Uman welcomes thousands of Hassidic pilgrims who come together to worship at the grave of Rabbi Nachman of Breslov on Rosh Hashana, the Jewish New Year.

The Crimean Tatars

Tatars are the historical inhabitants of the Crimean Peninsula who ruled Crimea until the Russian occupation in the eighteenth century. In 1944 the entire Crimean Tatar population was deported from Crimea to central Asia on Stalin's orders for alleged collaboration with the Nazis. A decree of 1967 cleared the Tatars of all charges; 260,000 Tatars have returned to Ukraine, and around half have been granted Ukrainian citizenship. However, the government cannot provide enough housing and jobs for such a massive influx of population. The Tatars, who constitute 12 percent of the population of Crimea, demand jobs and accommodation, compensation for their deportation, and the establishment of Crimean Tatar autonomy. The social and political situation in Crimea remains tense.

ATTITUDES TOWARD FOREIGNERS

Until the 1990s ordinary Ukrainians were actively discouraged by the KGB from having any contact with Westerners. In fact, one could lose one's job or be expelled from university for befriending a foreign tourist. Foreigners were approached with suspicion and curiosity.

In the first years after Ukrainian independence, many opportunistic Western entrepreneurs flocked into the country in search of a quick profit. Such ventures often backfired—particularly as, in return, the Ukrainians often regarded the foreigners as a source of easy income!

This, however, has been changing over the last twenty years as a result of the large number of foreign banks and companies working in the country and the thousands of Ukrainian students studying abroad. Ukrainian companies often invite Western managers to help them improve corporate governance and introduce good business practices.

As English is the main foreign language taught at school, a fascination with everything "British" ranges from the latest news about the royal family to the score of the recent Arsenal–Manchester United football match. Ukrainians often surprise British visitors with their knowledge of brands of tea, or quotations from *Hamlet*.

CLASS AND MONEY

The times, described by George Orwell, when "all people are equal, but some are more equal than others," have gone. Or have they? The Soviet Communist *nomenklatura*—the politicians and the KGB, who ran the country—were replaced by a new government, which organized itself in a similar, Soviet-style hierarchy.

So, what's new? Ukrainian society has rapidly become stratified. Ukraine has got new classes—of superrich and beggars. The new Ukrainians, the superrich, flaunt their money. It is claimed that there are more new Mercedes cars in Kyiv than there are in Stuttgart where they are manufactured.

The *intelligentsia*—the professional class of teachers, doctors, and engineers—is so impoverished that your taxi driver may well be the former manager of a company, or a teacher in a technical school, trying to make ends meet.

Two-thirds of the Ukrainian "consumer basket" is taken up by food. However, even the high price of appliances and the uncertainties of the future do not stop Ukrainians from traveling. People use their savings or take "travel loans" provided by the banks. The wanderlust that has swept the nation can be explained by the fall of the Iron Curtain and the traditional Cossack spirit of adventure, along with the desire to provide the best possible vacations for the children—Ukrainians would rather spend money on the education and leisure of their offspring than on themselves.

THE UKRAINIAN SOUL

A country that does not keep its heritage loses its identity. Pagan roots, proximity to nature, and attempts to capture natural beauty fostered Ukraine's spiritual traditions, which have been passed down through generations.

The Artistic Temperament

The strong bond between Ukrainians and nature is reflected in art. From ancient times the *hatas* (peasant houses) had walls, cups, boxes, trunks——everything used in everyday life—decorated with floral and animal patterns. If you go to a Ukrainian village today, you will see tidy, flower-filled gardens, carved gates, and painted walls. The desire to decorate is still strong. The traditional Ukrainian *sorochky* (shirts) have an embroidered symbolic black and red Tree of Life on them. The *pysanky*— painted wooden Easter eggs— have a huge range of patterns and colors. These painted eggs are so popular that Ukraine hosts the world's only museum of *pysanky* at Kolomyia in Western Ukraine, where the main hall, approaching forty-three feet (about thirteen meters) high, is built in the shape of an egg.

There is a traditional artistic reference in the wedding ceremony, when the bridesmaids spread an embroidered towel (*rushnik*) on the floor. Whichever of the newlyweds steps on it first will be the head of the family. The towel must not contain black or yellow  threads, as these colors symbolize death or separation.

Melancholy

Centuries of tragic history and the challenges and instability of the new state have taken their toll on the people. Ukrainian melancholy manifests itself in the recurrent criticism of everything, from the government to the snow, and in the compulsion to describe all one's minor ailments to an interlocutor in response to the simple greeting, "How are you?" Complaining is a national pastime.

"The Singing Nation"

According to a Ukrainian folktale, God one day heard crying at his door. He looked out and saw a little girl. "Why are you crying, child? " asked God. "You were giving presents to the other children, God, and I was late. I didn't get anything," was the reply. "All right," replied God. "I shall give you a present that I was keeping for myself." And he gave the little girl a song. Her name was Ukraine.

Ethnographers have collected around 36,000 Ukrainian songs. Many folk songs are used in modern remixes, and sung by young and old alike. Even Ruslana, the Ukrainian winner of the forty-ninth Eurovision Song Contest in Istanbul in 2004, used the traditional ethnic melodies of the Carpathian Mountains in her effervescent performance. As a result, in 2005 the fiftieth Eurovision Song Contest was hosted by Kyiv .

Bandura

The most popular Ukrainian folk instrument is the *bandura*. It was preceded by a stringed instrument called a *kobza*. The legendary *kobzars*, seventeenth-century wandering musicians, were the narrators and participants in long, lyrical ballads about historic events. They enjoyed such popularity and influence with the Cossacks that foreign invaders would torture them to death for lifting Cossack spirits and retelling the Cossack legends. The *bandura* is enjoying a revival in modern Ukraine, and *bandura* musicians are sometimes to be seen and heard on busy street corners.

RELIGION

Ukraine has more than a thousand years of Christian tradition. However, according to national statistics, until 1991 only 15 percent of the population considered themselves religious. This figure rose to 70 percent in a census of 2001. There are several reasons for this. The Soviet state pursued a policy of aggressive atheism. In 1926 religion was prohibited by law, and people could be prosecuted for going to church, or celebrating baptisms and religious holidays. Most weddings took place in register offices.

After the collapse of Communism, in a time of economic chaos, many people found solace in religion—it filled the vacuum that followed the crash of Soviet ideals, and gave hope and support. Ukrainian spirituality, suppressed during the Soviet era, found its release in religion. A significant number of monasteries were restored, and new churches are being built everywhere.

The divisions of the Church reflect the complex history of Ukraine. The disputes of recent history have separated the Ukrainian Orthodox Church, according to allegiance, into the Moscow and the Kyiv Patriarchates, with 75 percent of worshipers in Ukraine attending the Orthodox churches of the Moscow Patriarchate. The Ukrainian Autocephalous Orthodox Church is self-governing, with 80 percent of worshipers practicing in the western part of the country.

The Ukrainian Greek Catholic Church was outlawed in 1946 and emerged from the underground in 1989. It follows the Byzantine rite, and the architecture is similar to that of the Orthodox Church, but it recognizes the supremacy of the Pope. In addition, there is a significant presence of Roman Catholics, Protestants, and a number of new religious movements whose missionaries entered Ukraine after independence, looking for converts.

It is worth visiting a church in Ukraine to admire the ornate décor inside, and to watch Ukrainian spirituality coming to life. You will find representatives from all walks of life there.

Respectable businessmen and lanky teenagers in leather jackets put candles in front of the icons; middle-aged women listen to the liturgies, whispering prayers. When visiting Orthodox churches, women cover their heads with scarves, and men remove their hats. Worshipers stand during Orthodox and Greek Catholic services, which are conducted in the old Slavonic language, apart from the services of the Ukrainian

Church of the Kyivv Patriarchate and the Ukrainian Autocephalous Church, which are conducted in Ukrainian. The services are beautiful, moving, and very long (one is allowed to leave during them).

SUPERSTITIONS

Ukrainian everyday life is entangled in a cobweb of unspoken rules. Paganism, practiced before the tenth century, regular observations of nature, and the Ukrainian love of mysticism have led to many superstitions. During your visit you will encounter superstitious habits and protocol from the first greeting to your departure.

For a start, don't shake hands across the threshold. Don't whistle in the house, and don't keep your empty bottles on the table. All will bring bad luck. You will have a bad day if you have forgotten something and have to return for it, but will be extremely lucky if you sit between two people with the same name. Oh, and don't forget to sit down for a moment of silence before anyone leaves on a journey, as a gesture to the departing for a quick and safe return.

Most mothers attach a safety pin to their children's clothes to ward off the evil eye. Everybody, from an old man to a schoolgirl, will spit three times across their left shoulder if a black cat crosses the road.

The proud Kyivites will tell you that the Bare Mountain in Kyiv is one of only three places in the world where witches gather for a Sabbath.

There was a talk show on national Ukrainian TV called *The Life of Things*, about "unhappy" mirrors, pianos, and pictures that were creating havoc in the lives of their owners. The experts on the show gave advice on the "biological cleansing" and taming of the misbehaving objects.

Extra Time

A Ukrainian centenarian broke a mirror, and was overjoyed. "Why are you so happy?" asked his friend. "Doesn't breaking the mirror bring seven years of bad luck?" "Of course it does—but it's a whole seven years!" he replied.

HEALING

Folk medicine is an integral part of Ukrainian life. People continued to follow pagan healing traditions long after the arrival of Christianity. The absence of good medication during Soviet times led to the preference even by urban, educated people for natural remedies rather than antibiotics. Newspapers that give advice on self-treatment and healing are second in popularity only to publications on astrology and mysticism.

If you so much as sneeze in the office, you may be offered a tincture of onion juice and honey; or a garlic paste; you will be advised that cottage cheese or a goat lard wrap will help a chest infection. You will be told to drink tea spiked with honey, vodka, and lemon juice at bedtime. The home remedy advice will be endless, and even contradictory, but it will have one factor in common—all the ingredients are natural.

While Westerners may think of Ukrainians as hypochondriacs, and view such remedies as nothing but old wives' tales, the counterargument they hear is that "a creaky oak won't fall for a long time." The common view is that as natural remedies cause no harm, they are a good preventive measure.

chapter three

HOLIDAYS & FESTIVALS

NATIONAL HOLIDAYS

The Ukrainian generosity of spirit is evident in the inclusive way they enjoy their celebrations—you will always be invited to join in. The holiday calendar provides many opportunities for this.

State holidays, marked red in calendars, are official days off. They are a mixture of the legacy of Soviet celebrations, holidays introduced after independence, and the revival of Orthodox festivities.

PUBLIC HOLIDAYS	
January 1	New Year's Day
January 7	Orthodox Christmas
March 8	International Women's Day
Movable	Easter
May 1	Festival of Spring
May 9	Victory Day
Eighth Sunday after Easter	Trinity
June 28	Constitution Day
August 24	Independence Day

January 1: New Year's Day

According to a recent survey, this is the favorite Ukrainian holiday. This is not surprising, as it is the only holiday unaffected by politics or religion. Both Eastern and Western astrology have their place here, and the newspapers are full of advice on what to wear and which dishes to put on the table to welcome the New Year.

The festive celebrations begin with tree-decorating and exchanging gifts on New Year's Eve. Did Moroz, a version of Santa Claus, and his blonde granddaughter Sniguronka, the Snow Maiden, bring presents.

There is a saying that however you welcome the year is the way you will spend it, so the tradition is to have a big celebration, with fanfares, fireworks, and enthusiastic partying through the night.

January 7: Orthodox Christmas

In the seventeenth century most European countries adopted the Gregorian calendar. Russia adopted it only in 1918, but the Orthodox Church did not. Christmas, Easter, and Trinity are therefore celebrated according to the Julian calendar, thirteen days later.

Celebrating Orthodox Christmas was forbidden under the Soviet regime (and was resurrected officially only at the end of the 1990s). However, many families still gathered for *Sviata Vecheria* (Holy Supper) on January 6. This meal consists of twelve meatless courses, each dedicated to one of Christ's twelve apostles. The first traditional dish is *kutia* (a sweet soup with poppy seeds, honey, nuts, and barley). Stuffed cabbage, dumplings, fish, and *borshch* are also served. Masked children go from door to door, singing *kolyadki* (Christmas carols) and wishing good health and happiness.

March 8: International Women's Day

If you are buying flowers on this day, beware of the prices—they will be sky-high—but you will hardly see a woman on the street without a bunch of tulips or roses. Men give chocolates, flowers, and small gifts to their wives, mothers, daughters, sisters, and female friends and colleagues. Ironically, as men like to celebrate as well, the women still end up doing all the cooking!

Easter

The preparations for Easter start three weeks in advance. With the resurgence of religion in the country many people observe Lent, and fast. Three days before Easter is "Clean Thursday," when everything in the home should be cleaned.

Many people attend church on the Saturday evening. The service starts at 11:30 p.m. and lasts until 4:00 a.m. In recent years it has been broadcast on TV and attended by political leaders. The Orthodox priest greets the congregation with the words, "Christ is risen!" and the congregation replies in chorus, "Indeed He is risen!" and exchange triple kisses.

During the day people visit relatives and close friends and present them with Easter baskets, filled with blessed *paskhas* (Easter cakes) and *pysanky* (Easter eggs). The Ukrainian Easter egg fight is similar to the Greek one: after the festive dinner, everyone tries to break the egg of the person next to them.  The one whose shell remains intact will be the luckiest throughout the year.

May 1: Festival of Spring
This day is a legacy of Soviet times, when it was one of the greatest holidays of the year, with grand parades and propaganda banners. Although it is no longer celebrated as International Workers' Solidarity Day, or Labor Day, it retains its festive spirit, with people going to the parks and countryside for *majivky*—barbecue and picnic celebrations. May 2 is also an official holiday.

May 9: Victory Day (in the Great Patriotic War)
Almost every Ukrainian family suffered losses in the
Second World War, and this is a day for remembering
the veterans, who (fewer every year) wear their
uniforms and medals for the day, and meet their
friends in the parks. Military parades are held, and
wreaths are laid on the Tomb of the Unknown Soldier.

Trinity Sunday
Observed on the eighth Sunday after Easter, Trinity
Sunday is one of the most important religious
holidays, but has only recently become a state
celebration. For believers this is the day on which
the Holy Spirit descended upon the apostles. People
rejoice at the coming of new life by decorating their
houses and apartments with grass and wildflowers.
In the country, floors are covered with long grass; in
the city dried flowers are tucked behind pictures.

June 28: Constitution Day
On this day in 1996 the first Ukrainian Constitution
was adopted. This is a day off rather than a
celebration, and is used to raise patriotic awareness,
with frequent broadcasting of the Ukrainian anthem
on the radio.

August 24: Independence Day
On August 24, 1991, the Ukrainian Parliament
(Verkhovna Rada) declared Ukraine a sovereign

state. Every year the celebrations of this event include concerts on the main squares of the big cities, fireworks, and street parties.

OTHER CELEBRATIONS
Apart from official holidays, there are also a number of significant or special dates that may occasion celebrations in the evenings of regular working days.

January 13: Old New Year's Day
Before 1917 Russia and Ukraine, following the Julian Calendar, were thirteen days behind the rest of the world. However, even though the country switched to the Gregorian Calendar in 1917, many people refused to change their habits and continued to celebrate New Year as before. As a result, there are two New Year celebrations in Russia and Ukraine. Those on Old New Year's Day are not on such a grand scale as the ones on January 1, however, and it is not a day off.

January 25: Tatyana's Day, or Students' Day
In the eighteenth and nineteenth centuries this day was celebrated as the Day of Foundation of Moscow University, but in the second half of the nineteenth century it became a holiday for all universities and students—a celebration of the carefree days of youth. Current students and those of the previous decade take part.

February 14: St. Valentine's Day
This is a new, post-Soviet holiday, enjoyed by the younger generation and card manufacturers alike.

February 23: Former Red Army Day
Through conscription, 90 percent of men in the Soviet Union served in the Army. Although the Ukrainian Army has its own Army Day on December 6, in the absence of both Father's Day and the Soviet Army, the day developed into a celebration for all men. Most women give presents to their male relatives and friends.

April 1: April Fool's Day
The best way to celebrate April Fool's Day is to visit Odesa, which stages a comedy festival called "Yumorina." The inhabitants of Odesa are known in Ukraine for their particular kind of irony and dry humor, and many famous Soviet comedians came from there. Humor is everywhere in Odesa: there is a humor channel on the radio, the slogans in the streets are full of humor.

July 7: Ivana Kupala
This holiday, a festival of fire and water, was one of the most important pagan celebrations for the Slavs. The day is named after the pre-Christian god of water (Kupala) and John the Baptist (Ivan). The night of July 6 in Ukraine was always a

magical, mysterious night of rites and rituals using the two elements of fire and water. People light fires and keep them going all through the night, leaping over the flames to cleanse themselves of diseases and bad luck. The ashes are taken home for protection against evil forces. Herbs picked that night are said to have strong healing properties. At sunrise, young girls release garlands of flowers to float down the streams in search of husbands.

September 1: Day of Knowledge

This is the first day of the academic year. In every school, smartly dressed pupils bring flowers for their teachers. The new, first-year children gather for an inauguration assembly in the schoolyard. As part of this ceremony a first-year girl is carried on the shoulders of a graduating student, ringing the first bell, opening the Road to Knowledge.

November 7: Great October Socialist Revolution Day

Once a great Soviet holiday, with two days off, this day lost its political significance and ceased to be a public holiday in 2002; but you may still see some elderly Communists marching with red flags and banners, demonstrating for "the stability of the good old days."

December 25: Catholic Christmas
This day is celebrated in Western Ukraine with
all the usual Christmas traditions.

CHOOSE YOUR MEETING DATES CAREFULLY
With the New Year, Christmas, and Old New Year
celebrations lasting until mid-January, it is not
worth arranging meetings in the first two weeks
of the New Year.

In May, with three official days off (May 1, 2,
and 9) and the beginning of the *dacha* (country
house) season, many people will be away from
their offices until the third week of May.

Apart from all these holidays, every city has its
own special days. The best-known is that of Kyiv,
celebrated on the last weekend of May with open-
air art exhibitions, music, and snack kiosks. And,
as if this were not enough, there are also the
professional holidays, celebrated by those who
do particular jobs (for example, January 29 is the
firefighters' day, and July 11 is the fishermen's
day). Altogether there are eighty professional
holidays, and it seems that every year a profession
that does not already have its own celebration
applies for one!

Birthdays are big events in Ukraine—they are
celebrated not only at home, but also in the office,
with friends and colleagues. And this is not all. As

well as a birthday, everyone has an Angel's Day (the equivalent of a Saint's Day), which is often celebrated as a second birthday. It is called *Imenyny*, "name celebration." For example, June 20 is Maria's Day, and September 8 is Angel's Day for Natalya.

With so many holidays and celebrations it is not surprising that Ukrainians spend so much money on food. You are very likely to be invited to join in, and this is when another set of unpublished rules starts to operate. The way you behave at a party will either make or break your visit.

chapter four

MAKING FRIENDS

For Ukrainians, friendship does not just mean meeting someone for a regular pint in a pub or a weekly lunch date. Friends are considered to be part of the family. You can call a friend in the middle of the night if you need to, or turn up unannounced, and always count on his or her support. In Ukraine it will take you some time to make a real friend, rather than simply a social acquaintance, but be patient and you will be offered friendship and loyalty for life.

With Ukrainian traditions of hospitality and a considerable number of celebrations throughout the year, you are sure to be invited to at least one party, either in a private home or in a restaurant. The Ukrainian word *zastillya*, which means a celebration or a banquet, is translated literally as "at the table." It is over meals that friendships are forged and business deals are clinched.

It is not usual to send written invitations. The spontaneity and rapid changes of Ukrainian life don't allow for much long-term planning. An invitation by phone or in person will generally be issued with a few days' notice. An invitation immediately raises the usual questions, such as what to wear, and what to take. Here, then, is a brief overview of Ukrainian party etiquette.

PARTIES

"The Cossacks . . . were indomitable, like the rocks of the Dnieper among which they lived, and in their furious feasts and revels they forgot the whole world," wrote Mykola Hohol. So what sort of feasts and revels await you?

Time for Coffee!

A request to drop in at a friend's home for coffee, or to meet someone in a bar or a café, is usually spontaneous, and is an invitation to have a chat. Be warned, though, that if you are invited to "come for a quick coffee" one morning, it is very likely to be a soul-searching session, lasting well into lunchtime, and you will probably be fed—so plan your time accordingly!

Barbecues and Garden Parties

Ukrainians love the outdoors, and going out for a barbecue (*na shashlyky*) is their favorite activity.

The atmosphere will be quite informal, whether it is a picnic in the woods near the river or in the garden of someone's *dacha*. Wear jeans and T-shirts, not suits and hats. Such parties are a rare chance to observe the cooking skills of Ukrainian men, as grilling the meat (normally marinated overnight in red wine with spices) is considered a male activity. Though you'll be told "don't bring anything, just yourself," a bottle of wine will always be a welcome contribution.

Receptions and Buffet Parties

Fifteen years ago, in Soviet times, a reception was purely a diplomatic event, inaccessible to the majority of the population. Now many Ukrainian companies are holding receptions at inauguration ceremonies and product launches. These receptions are a curious combination of attempts to provide elite entertainment within Ukrainian traditions. A finger buffet is not a familiar event for Ukrainians, and the food served is often inappropriate—versions of *varenyky* (see page 109) with sauces; various pickles, and *salo* (pork fat) sandwiches. One leaves the reception either hungry or covered in drips and splashes.

For Ukrainians, to eat and converse while standing up and juggling a plate and a glass is not a real celebration.

Let's Have a Real Party!

A Ukrainian professor, on her return from a year's lecturing in the United States, decided to give a buffet party at home for her friends. After ten minutes of silent munching and standing next to the table by the wall, her friends moved the table to the center of the room and brought in the chairs. Only then did the conversation liven up and the party get going.

Wedding Receptions

Weddings are in a category of their own. A Ukrainian wedding is a great event to attend as it embodies many traditions, old and new.

The celebrations begin with the laying of flowers at one of the city monuments. This ceremony has its roots in the old Ukrainian tradition of visiting the "holy places" after the wedding. In the Soviet atheist state they were replaced by visits to the monuments of Lenin and the Tomb of the Unknown Soldier. Times change, and in Kyiv today couples visit the monument to the founders of the city. It was symbolic that, during the Orange Revolution in 2004, wedding parties came to the main square of Kyiv, covered in orange ribbons, and gave flowers to the demonstrators.

The *tamada* (toastmaster) runs the wedding reception. He invites the guests to speak, or to sing; he tells jokes, and recites poems. Ukrainians often say that the success of a wedding reception depends on the toastmaster.

Another wedding tradition is that of kidnapping the bride for a "ransom," such as a case of champagne, a bag of coins, or a song. Don't be surprised to see a bride with two "minders" in a hotel elevator—they will be hiding from the groom, who will be hurriedly getting the ransom ready in the hotel restaurant.

THE DINNER PARTY

It is at a sit-down dinner, the most traditional Ukrainian party, that the Ukrainian personality shines through. To attend a party of this kind, with the traditions of introductions, toasts, conversations, and even the consumption of the food, is a skill that needs understanding and practicing.

Imagine this scenario. Your Ukrainian colleague invited you to a dinner party at his home. When you arrived you shook his hand as he opened the door,

kissed his wife on both cheeks, and gave her four yellow chrysanthemums. You drank a little, politely refused a second helping of food, and left after listening to some songs sung by the other guests. You thoroughly enjoyed the evening, and you sent a little note of thanks. It is a complete mystery to you why your Ukrainian friend now avoids you in the office, and frowns every time he passes you in the corridor. What you don't realize is that your behavior at his party was a complete breach of the unspoken protocol of hospitality in the Ukrainian home.

The Ukrainian host would be pleased to see you, and would shake your hand—but not across the threshold! Don't ignore this Ukrainian superstition; step inside, and take your gloves off. And then, to avoid embarrassment, don't initiate the handshake yourself—follow the host. Handshakes are not obligatory, and if your host simply nods his head, that's enough for you too. Alternatively, if you are good friends, he may give you a hug.

Then, if you don't know your hostess well, don't kiss her. If she is a long-standing friend you can kiss her three times, both on arrival and on departure. This tradition comes from the Easter *hrystosuvannya*—a celebratory triple kiss. And don't kiss a woman or a child on the forehead—this is for funerals only.

As Ukrainians remove their shoes and change into slippers to keep their carpets clean, you might be offered a pair of slippers too, especially in winter, so make sure your socks are in order!

Gifts

If there are children in the family, they will expect you to bring something sweet. You can also bring a bottle of wine or whiskey for the host. Don't bring Ukrainian wine or *gorilka*. As a foreign guest, you will be expected to bring either something exotic or nothing at all.

Say It with Flowers

The Ukrainian love of nature is reflected in the love of flowers. Flowers are brought to birthday parties, presented to sweethearts on dates, and to teachers on the first and last days of a school year; they are a part of political celebrations and veteran homage. Flowers show joy on reunion at an airport or railway station, and are a symbol of loss and grief at funerals. In February, snowdrops and violets are sold on the streets as a sign of spring approaching.

In Ukraine, the symbolism of flowers can be a culture trap, as number, color, and type of flowers all carry a special meaning. There is no margin of error at all. The flower sellers will be happy to advise you.

The Meaning of Flowers

What seemed to be a promising courtship finished on the second date, when the young Englishman presented the Ukrainian girl with eight yellow chrysanthemums. What he didn't know was that an even number of flowers (often chrysanthemums or lilies) is for funerals only, and that yellow is the color of farewell. The girl saw the flowers as a sign that the new relationship was over.

If you are going to a birthday party, you should take an odd number of flowers—three, seven, or nine. Giving more than nine flowers indicates serious romantic feelings and intentions. However, if you want to splash out and present a birthday girl with as many flowers as she has years, you may have to add or subtract one to make an odd number. Not to present a bouquet of flowers to your girlfriend on International Women's Day is a deadly sin.

Apart from yellow flowers, which mean separation, both red and white flowers have their own meanings. White, a symbol of innocence, is appropriate for weddings, while red (especially in red carnations) is a symbol of victory and patriotism, and has political connotations. Red carnations can be presented to a man on an anniversary, or to a veteran on Victory Day. In

Soviet times no parade or political ceremony was complete without red carnations.

At the Table

Aperitifs are not common at Ukrainian parties, and you will be taken straight to a table covered lavishly with food. This is just for starters—literally, as these are *zakuski*, or appetizers. They will include various salads, pickles, and cold meats. The guests usually help themselves (and if you take something, you should eat it).

A Ukrainian housewife will think her guests are not enjoying themselves if they are not eating well . . . and eating more . . . and more. A nineteenth-century Ukrainian play, *Pan Khalyavsky*, describes a feast where the guests had to take their belts off after the first course and unbutton their shirts after the main dish, but the host was still anxious that they were hungry. Overfeeding guests is a national tradition, exacerbated by the fact that refusing food is considered rude.

When you finally reach the dessert (which is served with the tea or coffee), you will hardly be able to speak. But you must—because the guests are expected to make a toast to the hosts, to friendship, and to the cooking skills of the hostess before they depart. And they are expected to join in the singing as well!

Toasting

Ukrainians are earnest toastmasters, and the party is not a celebration without a series of toasts, which follow a strict hierarchy. The first toast is usually proposed by the host, either to the guests or to friendship. The third toast is traditionally to the women (or to absent friends, if you are a sailor). The men have to drink it to the full, standing up. The shortest and most popular Ukrainian toast is "*Budmo!*"—"Let us be!" Everyone makes their own wishes to end the main toasting—happiness, health, and so on. At the end of the evening the host proposes the final toast, "*Na konya!*" (literally, "On to the horse!"), to the departing guests. It is the Ukrainian equivalent of "One for the road!" and comes from the time when the Cossacks would have had a last drink before galloping away.

TO DRINK OR NOT TO DRINK

Society sees drinking as an integral part not only of celebration and relaxation, but also of everyday life. The Kyivan prince Vladimir remarked in the tenth century, "In Rus drinking is enjoyment and we cannot exist without it." Vodka, cognac, champagne, wine, and beers are drunk in Ukraine, but vodka and *horilka* are, without a doubt, the most popular drinks. The majority of prime-time TV advertisements in Ukraine are for different vodka and *horilka* brands. You can choose from "Vodka for real males," "Horilka for serious Ukrainians," "Vodka at its purest," and "Vodka, your understanding friend."

The most typical Ukrainian *horilka* is *medova z pertsem*—a strong spirit with a hot, spicy taste from the chili pepper in it, a slight bitterness of wild herbs, and a tinge of honey. It is attributed with many properties, from cold fighting to aphrodisiac. You will never know until you try it yourself.

If you don't drink, you may be regarded with suspicion, as a person who can't be trusted. If you want to retain your hosts' respect and not get drunk at the same time, you can use the state of your health as an excuse—you might be taking medication not compatible with alcohol. You will be understood and supported, but will have to listen to medical advice throughout the dinner.

TOPICS OF CONVERSATION
Apart from healing and health, there will be plenty of other topics of conversation at the Ukrainian dinner table, and some topics that should

probably be avoided. The weather, for example, is far too dull a subject!

Ukrainians love books, and conversations about recent novels, philosophy, and history are common. Ukraine has a 99.5 percent literacy rate. The daily papers form the largest part of the printed media—there are hundreds of newspaper and magazine titles—so it is not surprising that conversation  often reflects the newspaper columns and revolves around politics, economic developments, and sports. As the country is undergoing structural political change, everybody discusses politics. So don't be surprised if there is an ardent debate on what has just been said in Parliament.

Children and Family

Ukrainians see the achievements of their offspring as a priority, and parents often talk about their children with pride. They will show you proof of their academic triumphs and the trophy won at a recent sports competition; there will be a demonstration of musical talents; and so on. But they will not only talk about the children—they will discuss their families in general. Foreigners are often surprised at the way in which Ukrainians readily divulge to them the details of a family quarrel, or other such problems, along with their plans for the forthcoming wedding.

Soul Searching

Several toasts may bring on an extensive sentimentality session. Ukrainians are quite compassionate, and are often interested in, and prepared to listen to and sympathize with, somebody else's problems. They are often surprised by the existence of counseling services in other countries. "But what are friends for?" is a common question.

Money

The hyperinflation at the beginning of the 1990s, the collapse of pyramid financing scams, and the loss of personal savings have all made Ukrainians very knowledgeable about such topics as banks and interest rates. Prices are often discussed, but so also are salaries, so be prepared for direct questions: "How much do you earn?" "How much did you pay for your car/house?" It's not personal—just benign curiosity.

Age

It is not common to talk about age, especially a woman's age. Even at big celebrations of fiftieth, sixtieth, or seventieth birthdays, the age is not necessarily mentioned in the toasts. There is a

Ukrainian joke about three women at a dinner arguing about which of them was going to propose the next toast. The host made a suggestion: "Let the eldest begin." This was greeted with a stony silence.

Jokes

As there is no Ukrainian celebration without a toast, there is no celebration without a large measure of jokes and humor. Ukrainians are the masters of black humor—mainly because it helped people to survive the hard times and gave some respite from their worries. Apart from the universal jokes about infidelity and in-laws, there are jokes reflecting the realities of Ukrainian life: about vodka and excessive alcohol consumption, corrupt policemen who earn their living by charging bribes, and about "new Ukrainians" and "new Russians."

Close to the Bone . . .

- What is paradise? An American salary, an English house, a Ukrainian wife, and Chinese food. What is hell? A Ukrainian salary, a Chinese house, an American wife, and English food.
- "Peter," said Irina, "there will be three of us soon!" "I am so thrilled, darling," he replied. "I knew you would be," she said, "Mother is moving in with us next week!"

With the consuming interest in politics, there are endless jokes about the Soviet era and the new political leaders. However, though people will tell you political jokes, it would be seen as offensive if you, as a foreign guest, related a joke about Ukrainian politics.

As a guest, though, you will also be expected to contribute some jokes. Think up a few suitable ones in advance, and remember that cricket, golf, or baseball jokes, for example, will not be understood, as these sports are not popular in Ukraine and the rules are not generally known.

A Written "Thank You"?

Ukrainians would be at best surprised, at worst suspicious, if they received a note or card thanking them for their hospitality. They would consider it too formal, and they would wonder whether everything indeed went well.

Going with a Swing

A Ukrainian living in America wrote to his friend back home, "How we miss our parties in Kyiv, where we talked about eternal problems, argued, shouted, were force-fed, and got drunk, and loved. At parties here in New York conversation is about meaningless things, we eat buffet food if we want it, drink if necessary, and nobody forces us . . ."

One might find the Ukrainian party tradition excessive both in food and alcohol consumption and in emotional display, but it is an integral part of the culture, of bonding, and socializing.

KITCHEN TALKS

You'll know you've been accepted as a close friend when you're invited to have a meal in the kitchen. This originates from the Soviet era, when people would pop in to see a friend and find themselves sharing a meal and a bottle or two. During the Communist regime, when everybody was supposed to think and speak alike in praise of Communist Party achievements, real opinions were aired in the kitchen: it was a more intimate, less formal atmosphere, and people believed that their kitchens were less likely to be bugged!

chapter five

DAILY LIFE

Ukrainians don't smile at strangers on the street. They feel that smiles are for people they already like and care about. But once you get through the initial stage of solemn faces, you will discover that Ukrainians are spontaneous, outgoing, and demonstrative, and that the southern climate encourages a Latin temperament.

You often see mothers shouting at their children one minute and covering them with kisses the next. Also Ukrainians talk more loudly than the average Western European, and they sound more assertive as the pitch drops at the end of each phrase. What may seem, to an outsider, to be an argument is probably a perfectly ordinary conversation.

Ukrainians are both inquisitive and talkative. Don't be shocked if somebody else in the shop is interested in what you are buying, and starts advising you against buying a particular type of sausage, say, or if an elderly woman you pass in the street scolds you for not wrapping up warmly enough.

FAMILY LIFE

A recent Ukrainian book on family and business etiquette advises that, "harmony in the family can be provided through clearly defined family roles .... A woman is responsible for creating a comfortable home and a friendly psychological atmosphere in the family."

In Ukraine, women still traditionally provide child care and kitchen work (on top of working); men are supposed to bring home the bacon and do the DIY. The roles are so clearly defined that there is a story of a Ukrainian wife who burst into tears when her English husband tried to help her clear up after dinner. She thought it was his way of showing her that she was not performing her domestic tasks properly.

Despite the significant drop in living standards after independence, according to a recent Ukrainian sociological survey, only 1 percent of divorces happen for financial reasons. The major causes of divorce in Ukraine, according to the research, are incompatibility, the birth of sick children, working away from the family, jealousy and infidelity, and alcoholism or drug addiction. Around 78 percent of the men and 73 percent of the women who took part in the survey think that a mother should stay at home with the preschool children.

In Soviet times both husband and wife had to work to sustain the family budget; now many wives do not work. A nonworking wife has become a status symbol, showing that the family can live on the husband's income alone.

Children

The following story sums up the Ukrainian attitude to children. A Ukrainian woman walked into a pharmacy and said, "I need some medicine for my child. He has the flu." "How old is the child?" asked the pharmacist. "Twenty-seven—but to me he is still my baby." Children are doted on, often overdressed, and overfed. "Don't run, you'll sweat and catch a cold," is the most common phrase heard in the playground.

Many young people continue to live with their parents after their graduation from university, and

sometimes parents support their children financially until well into their thirties. If in the West children are brought up to be prepared to face the reality of life on their own and become independent, Ukrainian children grow up knowing that the family will support and protect them in times of hardship. However, this comes with a price tag. Parents often feel the need to interfere in the lives of their grown-up children, even well after their marriage. And if they are unhappy with their children's choice of spouse they consider it natural to show it. A large proportion of those who divorce in Ukraine under the category of "incompatibility" quote "the negative influence of parents or in-laws."

Ukrainian children receive a well-disciplined upbringing, with parents giving them little or no choice. "Respect your father as your teacher," says a proverb. The showing of traditional respect to parents was reinforced by the Soviet system of authority. Decisions from the top were not for discussion, but for implementation.

Although 67 percent of Ukrainians are urban dwellers, most families have rural roots, and it is common for children to spend long summer vacations with their grandparents or other relatives in the country.

EVERYDAY ROUTINES
Family Meals

Ukrainians traditionally prefer hot baked and stewed food to cold snacks. For centuries Ukrainian Cossacks carried small cooking stoves with them to cook hot food while on the march.

Breakfast, especially for children, may be hot cereal such as porridge or buckwheat *kasha*, omelette with sausage, or *syrnyky*, little cheese pies.

At lunchtime, soup is a must, but if it cannot be eaten in the office or at school, it is served at home as a starter for dinner. There are hundreds of soup recipes in Ukraine, but *borshch* is the father of all

Ukrainian soups. Often known in the West simply as "beetroot soup," *borshch* in fact is quite sophisticated fare. Ukrainian housewives still test the "domestic goddess" skills of their future daughters-in-law by their ability to cook *borshch*. It is a version of minestrone, enriched with beetroot for color and sweetness. Some recipes list up to twenty ingredients, including pork, broad beans, mushrooms, and various other vegetables.

Ukrainians, like many Slavic people, see the warm kitchen as the center of family life. "Come, have something to eat!" are the first words of greeting for children coming home from school, husbands returning from work, or anyone coming home.

Everyday Shopping
It is no surprise that food shopping consumes a significant part of the family budget. Food shops open at 8:00 or 9:00 a.m. and stay open until 8:00 p.m. Most of them are open on Sundays too. Some shops close for one-hour lunch breaks. There are many private corner shops open until 11:00 p.m. or even twenty-four hours a day.

Modern supermarkets are opening on the outskirts of cities, and a Saturday supermarket shopping trip is becoming increasingly common.

Happily, gone are the days of the empty Soviet food shops, with long lines of people and nothing but canned fish on display. The Ukrainian food-processing industry was among the first to get a taste of the market economy, and the choices now available confirm Ukraine's "Breadbasket" status. People have an "as and when" approach to shopping, buying fresh food such as dairy products, bread, and ham several times a week. The reason for this is not only the abundance in the shops, but also that most Ukrainian food products have no preservatives, and as a result milk turns sour and bread becomes stale very quickly. Apart from the universal milk and yogurts, there are some dairy products that are distinctly Ukrainian—like *syrky*, which are small, chocolate-covered cottage cheese pieces stuffed with jam or nuts, and *ryazhanka*, which is cream, slowly oven baked in a clay pot.

Ready-prepared food is the Ukrainian answer to McDonald's, and delicatessen departments selling home-style salads, pickles, fried fish, baked meats, and pies are very popular.

The *Rynok*

Ukrainians cannot imagine shopping for food without a visit to the *rynok*, or food market. The food here is more expensive than in the shops, and is considered fresher and better quality. You can buy anything from organic eggs and honey to various vegetables and fruit. Since the Chornobyl disaster all fresh produce for the market is checked for radiation and certified. All green vegetables and fruit are safe to eat.

Again, there are many typical Ukrainian products sold here—cottage cheese, cut by a knife, sour cream, *salo* (raw or smoked pork fat), and row upon row of pickles. Sampling the pickles can be a very pleasant experience. Ukrainians pickle all sorts of vegetables and fruit for the long winters, from gherkins and *Sauerkraut* to marinated apples. When the former British prime minister John Major came to Ukraine in 1996, he visited the Bessarabka market in 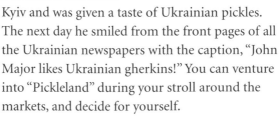 Kyiv and was given a taste of Ukrainian pickles. The next day he smiled from the front pages of all the Ukrainian newspapers with the caption, "John Major likes Ukrainian gherkins!" You can venture into "Pickleland" during your stroll around the markets, and decide for yourself.

WORK

The typical working day starts at 9:00 a.m. and finishes at 6:00 p.m. It is common in private companies to hold early management meetings at 8:00 a.m.

Lunch is taken between 1:00 and 2:00 p.m. A sandwich lunch is not common, and office workers try to eat hot food, preferably soup. "Dry food will cause a stomach ulcer," your colleagues will inform you every time they see you having a sandwich.

The Ukrainian women's magazine *Natali* informs us that 80 percent of its readers—working women in their thirties—are either regularly late for work or leave work early. The reasons, which are commonly accepted by their bosses, are "child's/spouse's/parent's illness" and "picking up the child from nursery/school."

EDUCATION

Child care and education were always the pride of the Soviet state system. In Ukraine, kindergartens were subsidized by the state or were supported and owned by factories and other industrial enterprises. In the 1990s more than 97 percent of preschool staff had degrees in preschool education. Since independence there has been a reduction in the kindergarten network due to lack of funds in the budgets of the enterprises, the decline in the birthrate, and extended periods of unemployment among parents. The temporary closure of nurseries has become a regular occurrence.

The situation improved when kindergartens were brought under municipal control. There is also a large number of private nurseries that charge much higher fees. Ukrainians favor nurseries over nannies and day-care providers, especially for the four- and five-year-olds. It is considered that the relatively structured regime in the nurseries, consisting of at least two hours a day of fresh air, art and music classes, and a two-course lunch, followed by a sleep, is a good preparation for primary school. Also, children can be picked up from the nursery as late as 7:30 p.m. If the parents are working late, the staff will stay with the children as long as necessary.

School
Ukraine inherited the rigid Soviet system of education, where the main principle was "collective development," and punishment was more frequent than praise. The Ukrainian Law on General Secondary Education introduced European standards—a twelve-year duration of study and an appropriate curriculum—and set up new examination requirements.

Schooling at a secondary comprehensive school begins at the age of six or seven years. There are twelve grade marks (8–9 is "Good"). The academic year lasts from September 1 to May 25, with several holiday breaks throughout the year. Apart from the state secondary schools, there are a number of private schools (including two international schools in Kyiv), but they have only been functioning for a little more than two decades. As a rebellion against the old drab brown Soviet uniforms, most schools now have no uniforms at all.

The school day starts at 8:30 a.m., ending at 12:10 p.m. for the first-years and at 2:10 p.m. for the rest. Many schools run optional after-school clubs. Ukrainian children are expected to do around about two and a half hours of homework every day. Most children participate in extracurricular activities, with football, tennis, swimming, ballet, music, and martial arts being the most popular.

Higher Education

Ukraine's State Higher Education System includes vocational schools, colleges, institutes, musical conservatories, academies, and universities, the majority of which are public. Nonpublic HEIs are controlled by the state through licensing and accreditation.

Half of all students are subsidized, and study free; the other half pay tuition fees. The irony is that often the nonpaying students still end up paying a lot in contributions to university funds or to line the pockets of certain dishonest tutors, who help them to get in.

The price of education depends on the rating of the university. The tuition fees for Kyiv University, for example, are among the highest.

After three years of studying for the baccalaureate, students either do the masters program for two years, or study for an additional year to become a "specialist."

MILITARY CONSCRIPTION

According to official figures, the Ukrainian armed forces employ some 355,000 people, of whom 265,500 are military personnel and 89,500 are civilian employees. The services face enormous challenges. Since independence the number of military personnel has been reduced five times, and there is a tendency to move toward a professional army. This will be achieved by slowly reducing conscription, which is currently set at the age of eighteen. Students in higher education are exempt. Until 2015 there will be a mixed system— conscripts will serve in the army for twelve months and in the navy for eighteen, and professional servicemen will sign up for three to five years.

Didovshyna, bullying and beating of recruits by senior conscripts, sometimes resulting in the death or suicide of the young soldiers, still exists as a legacy of Soviet times. Many Ukrainian boys are now willing to serve in the army, unlike in Soviet times, when joining up was a duty. In general, boys from rural backgrounds join the army for economic stability and security; urban boys join up to keep fit and have a macho image.

Ukrainian mothers are less worried about their soldier sons than Russian mothers, as there is no Chechnya and no internal terrorism or threat to the soldiers.

The Professional Army

Ukraine is one of the ten contributing nations to the UN's worldwide peacekeeping operations, and has been playing an increasingly large role. Since independence, about 37,000 Ukrainian servicemen have taken part in UN peacekeeping missions. Since 1997, Ukraine has been working closely with NATO, and especially Poland. A Ukrainian unit was deployed in Iraq, as part of the multinational force there under Polish command. Ukrainians see this service as a step up both socially and financially, and there are many applicants to join up.

WEEKEND ACTIVITIES

The weekend activities of Ukrainians can be divided into three categories: *dacha, na pryrodu* ("out to nature"), and "Sunday male."

Dacha

As Ukrainians say, "The *dacha* is not a hobby, it's a way of life." The interest in rose bushes and strawberries, apple harvest and frost-resistant seeds can be compared only to the British love of gardening. In Soviet times, the *dacha* was one of the perks invented by the system for the "equally poor." A state would allocate a plot of land to a factory or research center, and the managers would decide who deserved a *dacha* with a standard 0.6-acre plot. As a result of this land distribution, many Ukrainians could own their *dachas* without effectively paying for them. Most of these *dachas* are now privately owned. The difference between these old-fashioned plots and the new Ukrainians' three-story villas nearby is stark. And a green lawn around a country house means that the owners can afford not to grow their own vegetables.

Na Pryrodu

Na pryrodu, or "out to nature," includes various activities such as visiting relatives in the country, day or weekend hiking trips, fishing, and, in summer, sunbathing along the riverbanks. Go-carting and paint-balling are popular with teenagers.

The Sunday Male

This term describes a man on the sofa with a newspaper, with the implication that a woman is cleaning around him and doing the weekly chores. He will occasionally get up from the sofa so that his wife can vacuum it too, or so that he can exchange the newspaper for the TV remote control. His communication with his family can be described by this joke: " A Sunday Male relaxes on the sofa, watching the football on TV. His daughter runs to him; "Daddy, I am playing with my dolls!" The father replies (still watching TV), "Great! And who's winning?"

SPORTS

Ukrainians take sports seriously. The nation remembers that it can be a matter of life and death. In August 1942 the Ukrainian soccer team called "Start" (which consisted of players from Dynamo Kiev and other Soviet teams) played the famous "Match of Death" with Flakelf, a team of German soldiers. The Ukrainian players went against orders and refused to give a Nazi salute. They won 5–3. Four players were executed for disobedience. A granite monument to those players is located at the Dynamo stadium in Kyiv. The story of this occasion, told and retold over the years, has changed to become a famous legend about "the team who were killed for winning."

The brothers Vitaly and Vladimir Klitchko, both world heavyweight boxing champions, are respected not only as sportsmen, but also as businessmen and active supporters of children's charities.

Though Ukrainians would rather watch and discuss sports than participate, playing soccer and volleyball are popular ways of keeping fit. Billiards, both the Russian and American forms, is considered a high-status pastime for businessmen. Russian billiards is played with one-color balls, and the corner nets are much smaller.

Chess is a favorite game, and some parks have special areas for chess lovers. Most games are played for serious money, and the crowds gather to watch rather than play. Ukraine has had its share of chess fame.

Practically everybody plays cards on the beach, and men often organize overnight poker sessions—frowned upon by their wives.

Ukraine is co-hosting the Euro 2012 Championship and Ukrainians see this event as much more than a football tournament. It is the country's second chance since independence, after hosting the Eurovision contest, to show the world that Ukraine is a truly European country.

chapter six

TIME OUT

The way Ukrainians spend their free time varies according to age and how much money they have in their pockets: from gardening at the *dacha* to dancing the nights away; from fishing for fun or for food to eating out; from strolling in the open air to visiting the innumerable small and large galleries and museums.

Ukraine offers you plenty of choice. Young people enjoy the variety of nightclubs, expats favor the Western-style bars and pubs, families mainly choose outdoor activities, and the older generation strolls in the park.

More than 1,500 years of history have made Ukraine an archaeological paradise. The Carpathian Mountains offer Alpine skiing in winter, and the Mediterranean climate at the Black Sea provides great opportunities for a beach vacation. So, if you have any time left after the partying, start exploring.

You can begin with the country's main square in Kyiv. Maidan Nezalezhnosti (Independence Square) has become world-famous since the

Orange Revolution in November 2004. It was redesigned relatively recently, in 2001. Several ambitious sculptors jostled to leave their mark there, with mixed results; after walking around the square you will soon notice that they all had quite different tastes. On weekends and holidays, the square, the main street, Khreshchatyk, and the Podil district are closed to traffic and full of cheerful families, young couples, and groups of friends. Sometimes there are concerts or fireworks.

PARKS

The capital of Ukraine has the largest number of hectares of parkland per resident in Europe. A green swathe stretches along the slopes of the right bank of the Dnipro. Chestnut trees are an integral part of Kyiv, and the city's emblem is a chestnut bloom. Those finishing high school traditionally go to the parks to welcome the sunrise after their graduation parties at the end of May. The favorite place is the Lilac Garden in the Ukrainian Academy of Sciences Botanical

Garden, with its amazing collection established over fifty years ago.

Ten minutes by metro from the center of Kyiv is the Hydropark, with its sandy beaches, tennis, sailing, restaurants, nightclubs, and casinos.

Sofiyivka

Near the town of Uman, 130 miles (210 km) south of Kyiv, is Sofiyivka, the most aristocratic and romantic Ukrainian park. Built by the Polish count Stanislaw Potocki as a present for his Greek wife, Zofja (Sofia), it was opened on her birthday in 1802. The project was directed by Ludwig Metsel, a Polish military engineer who had traveled around Europe, visiting Versailles, Blenheim, and other famous parks, and decided that his creation "would outshine any other park in Europe." Eight hundred serfs worked for six years to complete it, and the waterfalls, gazebos, and classical statues of Sofiyivka have enchanted visitors ever since. The park was voted one of the Seven Wonders of Ukraine in 2007 by experts and the Internet community.

MUSEUMS AND GALLERIES
Lavra

The golden domes of Orthodox churches on the green banks of the Dnipro form what is often the first view of Kyiv to greet visitors coming from

the airport. These are the churches of Pechersk Lavra, the oldest monastery in Ukraine and a Unesco World Heritage Site. An active monastery and a theological academy, it also houses several museums.

The monastery is built over a network of caves, where the bodies of hermit saints have remained intact. The guidebooks tell you that the reasons for this are the ventilation of the caves and the sandy composition of the soil. But for the thousands of pilgrims arriving at Lavra every day to see the "holy bones," this is still a miracle. You can join them with a candle and walk around the underground churches in the caves.

On the brighter note, you can chose from the Museum of Historical Jewelry, with its unique collection of Scythian pieces, the Museum of Ukrainian Folk Art, the Museum of Books and Printing, and the amusing Museum of Miniatures, where through a microscope you can view a flea fitted with "horseshoes" and a golden rose finer than a human hair.

Mystetskyi Arsenal

The recently opened Mystetskyi Arsenal is a huge new art museum complex in Kyiv's historic eighteenth-century military arsenal building. By far the biggest arts and culture project in Ukraine, it hosts major exhibitions and cultural events, and in May 2012 was the venue for Kyiv's Inaugural International Biennale of Contemporary Art.

Pyrohiv

If you come to Ukraine for a short visit, it is possible to see the whole country in one day. In fact, you don't even have to leave Kyiv to visit a Carpathian village or to attend a religious service in a wooden church, typical of Eastern Ukraine. All you have to do is take a taxi to Pyrohiv, the State Museum of Folk Architecture and Daily Life of Ukraine. Houses, churches, windmills, taverns, and schools are arranged in settlements from various parts of the country. These are the original buildings, moved to the museum piece by piece and reassembled. The oldest *khata*, or whitewashed thatched cottage, in the museum dates back to 1587.

Various craftsmen, such as blacksmiths, potters, and weavers, demonstrate the old methods of their forebears. Traditional Ukrainian food is cooked in the *shynok*, a village tavern. As the museum is the largest of its kind in Eastern Europe, allow yourself a whole day there. If you are tired of walking, you can ride around on a horse, in true Cossack spirit.

Unusual Museums
Ukraine has a number of unusual museums. There is, for example, the dramatic Chornobyl Museum in Kyiv, which re-creates the feel of the site of the nuclear plant catastrophe with crumpled metal and "contaminated" signs, photographs of disfigured animals, and firefighters' uniforms.

You might also like to visit the underground Museum of Water, with an artificial thunderstorm, Kyiv's largest toilet, and a walk-through sewage tunnel, with realistically squeaking (plastic) rats.

Andriyivsky Uzviz

Ukrainians love art, and, apart from the well-established museums of Russian, Western European, and Ukrainian art, there are many modern galleries. Small art shops and galleries are clustered at the Andriyivsky Uzviz, often called the Kyiv Monmartre. This a cult street for Kyivites and visitors, and a heaven for street artists and souvenir traders. A street market comes into its own on weekends, holidays, and particularly on the Day of Kyiv, the last Sunday in May.

This cobbled street, in the shape of a gigantic "S," has from ancient times linked the upper part of the town, the administrative and religious center, with Podil, the "lower town," where the merchants and artisans lived. So many events of Ukrainian history and cultural life took place here that there is a "Museum of One Street" dedicated to the notable people who lived and worked here.

LEISURE SHOPPING

Andriyivsky Uzviz is wonderful for souvenir shopping, if you are not concerned with authenticity or fine detail. You can also buy embroidery, carved wooden boxes, and ceramics in the specialized "salons," where a certificate of authenticity is given with your purchase.

If you would like a taste of Soviet-style shopping, you can pop into "TSUM," the central department store in Kyiv, or any state department store in other Ukrainian cities, to experience "service without a smile." These shops are a stark contrast to the upmarket clothes boutiques that are popping up in the big cities, where you can find all the leading international brands. Ukrainians prefer to buy brightly colored clothes in the latest fashions, both as a reaction against the drab clothes of Soviet times and as a reflection of their southern tastes.

Book markets are extremely popular. There are two in Kyiv alone, each with over a hundred stalls.

The nonfood shops are open from 10:00 a.m. to 8:00 p.m., often throughout the weekends as well. Not all of them take credit cards, so it is a good idea to have some cash on you.

"What Should I Take Home"

The Orthodox Chants CD by the Pechersk Lavra choir from the Lavra shop; Rushniks—the embroidered festive towels (whose colors and stitches contain hidden symbols of life, joy, love, and eternity); Dynamo Kyiv shirts from the souvenir shop of the Dynamo stadium, host to the Euro 2012 football championship. And don't forget a bottle of *horilka*, Ukraine's spicy vodka infused with chilli pepper, at the airport. Italians claim it is the best aphrodisiac.

"Underground Life"

The extensive metro network and the large number of underground street crossings have led to the development of an underground world of street musicians, flower and newspaper stalls, snack vendors, and video shops. You can't be said to have experienced the Ukrainian way of shopping if you haven't sampled this phenomenon. There is a huge underground center under the main square in Kyiv, its presence announced on the surface by a glass dome. Metrograd, an underground boutique city in Kyiv under Bessarabskaya Square, is also popular.

The *Rynok*

Do visit the food markets. They are an explosion of colors, sounds, and aromas. You will be offered a piece of cheese, a slice of apple, and some smoked ham, and after a couple of rounds of the stalls you might not need any lunch. If you want to see the best (and the worst) of Ukrainian nature, a visit to the *rynok* on a Sunday morning is a must. The best ones to visit for people-watching are Bessarabka in Kyiv and Pryvoz in Odesa.

A respectable Ukrainian shopper won't buy anything at the market without haggling. Try it!

CAFÉ SOCIETY

Cafés allow Ukrainians to combine their favorite activities: long, friendly chats about nothing and everything, and watching the world go by. Add to this the national love of pastries, and you'll understand why, with the first warmth of spring, a stroll along one of the main streets turns into a slalom between the explosion of multicolored umbrellas and plastic tables.

You will be amazed by the number of coffeehouses, French-style *patisseries*, or just corner tables at the local grocery stores, selling poppy seed, honey cakes, and cream cakes. *Kyivsky tort* is as famous in Ukraine as *Sachertorte* in Vienna. The recipe is such an open secret that anyone will tell you that it is made of meringues with hazelnuts. Ukrainians love both tea and coffee. As a rule, coffee becomes more popular the further west in Ukraine you go. And, if you are health-conscious (most Ukrainians are), you will enjoy the rosehip or Carpathian herb tea.

RESTAURANTS

A little more than two decades ago, hungry tourists in Ukraine had a choice between eating in hotel restaurants with very limited, bland menus and no service, and not eating at all. Since independence, the Ukrainian love of food and entertainment, harnessed to their entrepreneurial spirit, has produced rapid results. You can choose to eat quickly and cheaply, or experience a gastro-menu for astro-prices, but in either case you are likely to eat well. Restaurants usually open at 11:00 a.m. and close at midnight, though many have a "last client" policy, and the eateries at the nightclubs work around the clock. Making reservations is recommended, and though most places take credit cards, it is better to check in advance.

Restaurants serving the national dishes range from expensive, such as Tsarskoye Selo in Kyiv, where dishes are prepared according to the old recipes in a traditional Ukrainian oven, to mid-range, like Opanas, where you'll be served by men in red, full of Cossack spirit. Try their roasted wild boar or stuffed pike with honey vodka.

Relatively recently fast-food chains serving high quality reasonably priced food have sprung up in the major cities: Puzata Hata ("Tummy Hut"), Dva Gusya ("Two Geese"), and Shvydko ("Quickly"). Japanese food is also popular, along with Italian, Chinese, and French. But even a Chinese restaurant in Kyiv will have *borshch* on the menu!

Although a traveler can stumble over the cluster of consonants in *borshch* (the menu will tell you it is "beetroot soup with sour cream"), not to try it would be like not trying pizza or pasta in Italy. There are about thirty ways to cook and serve *borshch*. It can be made with meat stock or mushrooms, served cold in the summer, and as a special festive dish for Christmas. The availability of ingredients is seasonal, and in the spring housewives usually cook "green" *borshch* with young nettles, sorrel, beet leaves, and boiled eggs.

Have you ever tried ravioli stuffed with morello cherries? It not, don't despair—it is not the creation of a fashionable Italian chef, but a popular Ukrainian dessert— *varenyky z vyshnyamy*. *Varenyky*, a version of oversized ravioli, is a staple of Ukrainian cuisine. There are dozens of fillings, the most popular being potatoes, fried pork, cabbage, and cottage cheese.

Another interesting dish is *holubtsi*. Though the name can be translated as "dearest," or "little pigeons," there is no pigeon meat in them at all. *Holubtsi* are cabbage rolls stuffed with meat and rice, or vegetables and rice during Lent, and stewed in tomato sauce.

If you are feeling very adventurous, try *salo*, which is a type of hard pork fat, smoked and marinated, salted, and baked. Ukrainians and their *salo* are legendary. The Russians say that Ukrainians would share anything but their *salo*. It is not to everybody's taste, but a thin slice of it goes well

with *horilka*, as it lines the stomach in preparation
for burning it with alcohol!

And if you are thirsty, Ukrainian beer is cheap
and of good quality ("Obolon" is the most popular
brand). Or you can try *kvas*, a nonalcoholic
beverage with a wheatlike taste sold from small,
wheeled tanks in the summer.

TIPPING

Tipping in restaurants is common—usually
around 10 percent of the bill. If you are
paying with a credit card, add the tip in cash,
otherwise the waiter will never see it.

NIGHTLIFE

In Kyiv alone there are about eighty nightclubs
and discos of all kinds. There is
something for everyone, from a
billiard club for amateurs to casinos
and techno dance clubs. Most of the
clubs offer strip shows of different
levels of quality and decency. Some
shows are quite elaborate, with laser lights and
fireworks. The action usually begins around 11:00
p.m., and goes on all night.

Pubs are becoming increasingly popular with
both visitors and Ukrainians. O'Brien's, in Kyiv,

serves Irish and Ukrainian dishes, and you can play darts or watch sports on giant TV screens.

There are also more inventive and unusual good pubs and cocktail bars: from O'Boxers pub, which offers fans a viewings menu of international football, boxing, or other major sporting events, to the OK bar in Kyiv, with glass walls that allow you to people-watch and admire the Polish cathedral outside, with no set cocktail list—you choose the ingredients and create your own cocktail.

THEATER AND MUSIC

Ukraine has a network of "musical schools." These are afternoon schools for children, where studies last for eight years, and the pupils learn not just to play the instruments but also to understand music. As a result, many Ukrainians have a great love for and understanding of classical music, and chamber and symphony concerts are an essential part of cultural life. There are regular children's concerts (both with children performing and for child audiences) at the National Philharmonic House in Kyiv.

Ukraine is famous for its singers. The opera is well worth a visit, and the Odesa, Kyiv, and Lviv opera houses are renowned for their ornate baroque interiors. The Odesa opera house, for example, is considered to be the second-most beautiful theater in Europe after Vienna's.

If you speak Russian or Ukrainian, you can take your pick from around thirty theaters in Kyiv alone. There is at least one theater for dramatic productions in every big city in Ukraine; plays range from Chekhov to modern experimental French works. Kyiv also boasts the smallest theater in Europe, called "21"—there are twenty-one seats, and a staff of twenty-one.

Ticket prices are generally reasonable, but when internationally famous or Russian stars are appearing the prices can be sky-high.

SPORTS

Football (soccer) is the national sport. Most Ukrainians are fans, and proud of their country's achievements, and those who can afford it often follow their teams around. Even if you are not a fan, you should at least know the names of the top Ukrainian teams: Dynamo Kyiv, Shahtar Donetsk, and Dnipro (Dnipropetrovsk). There are thirty-one clubs in the Ukrainian football league.

Ukraine has invested a huge amount in the hosting of Euro 2012. One politician described the games' importance as follows: "If Ukraine does not get it right, it will throw the country back twenty years."

Other Sports

For Ukrainians appearance matters, and this explains why gyms are not only popular, but also very expensive. Monthly membership of an elite Kyiv gym can cost about US $500.

With several Ukrainian players competing in world-class tournaments, tennis is fast becoming a favorite sport in Ukraine. You can play for about US $5.00–10.00 per hour.

If you are brave, you can try a public swimming pool. The Dynamo pool in Kyiv is open-air, and you can swim there even when the temperature is 14°F (-10°C)! The water is heated, and a cushion of steam protects the swimmers from the cold.

chapter seven

TRAVELING

Traveling around Ukraine is not as daunting as traveling around its northern neighbor Russia, as the distances are not thatgreat. Ukraine is similar in size to France, and you can get almost anywhere by train, bus, or car.

You can spend a weekend in Lviv, the aristocratic capital of Western Ukraine, or travel south to Odesa, the most cosmopolitan city. If you like skiing, hiking, or trout fishing, take a trip to the Carpathian Mountains. If you prefer the slower pace of a beach vacation, visit the Crimean peninsula, which has a subtropical climate and the famous cities of Sevastopol and Yalta.

ARRIVAL

Most international flights land at Boryspil International Airport outside Kyiv. Unless you are prepared to book the VIP service and pay US $40 for a shuttle minibus transfer and have your luggage delivered to you by a porter, you will have to make a beeline for the immigration booths.

Citizens of the EU (including British citizens) are allowed to enter Ukraine without a visa for a visit of up to 90 days. The overall duration of any stay without a visa must not exceed 90 calendar days per 180 calendar days from the date of first entry to Ukraine.

An appropriate visa will be required if you are traveling to Ukraine for the purpose of employment, study, family reunion, immigration, and the like. You should obtain it in advance—  many foreigners mistakenly assume that a visa can still be issued on arrival. The immigration card, to be filled in (and signed) on arrival, is another important document—it is your "passport to freedom." Keep it safely during your stay, as you have to present it again on departure.

Old Soviet habits die hard, and the attitude of "punishment over praise" welcomes you at the border. The immigration officers perceive you not as a friendly and adventurous visitor, bringing funds into the country, but, in Stalin's words, as "an enemy of the state." Even if you have followed all the rules and your immigration card is in order, you will still feel uncomfortable under the X-ray glare of the customs officer.

Boryspil International Airport is 25 miles (40 km) from Kyiv, and if you are not being met you can take either a shuttle bus (leaving every forty minutes) or a taxi. You must get through a crowd of cowboy taxi drivers as you leave the airport. Assume an air of confidence, because they can spot a lost tourist a mile away. There is a taxi stand outside, and the trip should cost you around US $20. However, if you can arrange in advance to be met by a driver it could be safer and is often cheaper. Try not to buy anything or change money in the airport. Everything there is expensive.

GETTING AROUND

By Air

Domestic flights connect Kyiv with nine major cities in Ukraine. Internal flights operate both from Terminal B at Kyiv's Boryspil airport and also from another airport, Zhulyany, on the other side of Kyiv, so plan your transfer accordingly.

By Rail

Trains are the most reliable means of long-distance travel, although comfort and punctuality vary. Trains run every day to Moscow, St. Petersburg, Budapest, Odesa, and Lviv. There are connections to all major cities in Europe. You can book a ticket forty-five days in advance, and this is advisable if you want to travel to the south in August. Be ready to present your passport at the ticket counter.

Traveling by train may be your first taste of Ukrainian-style communal living. There are three levels of comfort or class for long-distance or night travel: *Spalny vagon,* or luxury sleepers, with two pullout beds; *coupés,* sleeping compartments with four berths; and last and definitely least, *platskarta,* with six hard berths along an open corridor. If you are traveling alone and book a ticket in the *coupé* class, you will be spending the night with three strangers—unless you can afford to take the whole compartment.

"The journey is halved with a good travel companion," a Ukrainian saying assures you. A good companion in the Ukrainian sense is someone who will talk to you and offer you home-made food throughout the journey. Following another piece of Ukrainian wisdom, "Leave home for a day, take enough bread for a week," there will be plenty of good things to share. The traveling companion will also entertain you with his or her life story for as long as you are prepared to listen.

Local services around the major cities are provided by *elektrychky*—electric commuter trains with hard benches and no amenities.

By Car

The conditions of the roads in Ukraine are generally not good, but continuous work is improving matters. The best expressways are the recently

DRIVING TIPS

- Ukraine is a zero-tolerance country, and the DAI can impose severe fines on the spot if you have been drinking alcohol.
- Ukrainians say, "A good driver is not the one who knows the Highway Code, but the one who can predict the fools on the road." Ukrainian drivers are often reckless and pushy.
- The official speed limits are 37 mph (60 kph) within the city limits—though in the Kyiv traffic you will often crawl—and 74 mph (120 kph) on the expressways.
- To avoid problems with the DAI, always carry your driver's license and car registration documents. The car must be equipped with a first-aid kit, a fire extinguisher, and an emergency stop sign.
- Maintain your distance from the car in front, especially if it has a "Y" learner-driver sticker. Most learners don't bother to display these, and if the driver has decided to do so, it probably means that he has few driving skills!
- When oncoming cars flash their head-lights, they are probably warning you about a road inspection or speed control checkpoint ahead.

completed section of the road to Odesa (previously the most dangerous expressway in the country) and the road to Boryspil International Airport.

Hiring a chauffeur-driven car is a better option than renting a car to drive yourself, and can often work out more cheaply. Apart from the driving, the chauffeur obviously takes care of maintenance, fuel, parking, and dealing with the DAI (traffic police inspectors), who have gained notoriety for their unpredictable behavior and propensity to take bribes.

Most European car-rental companies have offices in Ukraine, and some hotels also have cars for rent. If you really want to drive yourself, ensure that the contract permits long-distance driving—sometimes you are limited to within the area of the city.

Driving in Ukraine in winter can be a dangerous experience. While winters can be warmer than in Russia, snow that melts into a dirty brown mush by day will convert the roads into a hazardous skating rink by night.

By Bus

If you are on a tight budget, and comfort is not your top priority, you can travel between cities and towns by bus. Ukrainian buses, and small private shuttle buses called *marshrutka*, operate between the cities. Ukrainian buses also operate on a number of international routes.

By Water

Cruising is the ultimate way to travel from May to October. For speed, take the hydrofoil to travel to the cities along the banks of the Dnipro (from Kyiv to Cherkassy, Zaporizhya, Dnipropetrovsk, Kherson, and Odesa), or join one of the first-class cruise ships. There are also seven-day sea cruises following the Black Sea shoreline.

URBAN TRANSPORTATION

Taxis

You can recognize an authorized cab by the checkered sign on the roof. There are a number of official taxi stops around the big cities. You can also order a radio taxi by phone, round the clock. The office will tell you the model and number of the car that is picking you up.

In Ukraine, however, practically any car can be considered a taxi, and people hail private cabs in the street. It is cheaper to do this, but you should agree to the price in advance, and be aware of the risks of getting into a car with a stranger. The driver may turn you down if your destination is not convenient for him. Hitchhiking is also common practice.

The Metro

The metro is undoubtedly the quickest and most reliable way to get around. Three Ukrainian cities

have a metro system: Kyiv, Kharkiv, and
Dnipropetrovsk. The Kyiv metro is the deepest
in the world, and one of the most beautiful: the
central stations have chandeliers and marbled
walls. You pay with a pre-purchased token (in
Ukrainian, *zheton*) or you can buy a pass
(*proyiznyi*)—even though it is for a month, it is
only 95 hryvnas and is worth buying to avoid
standing in line for tokens. A single journey costs
2 hryvnas, irrespective of distance. One token also
allows for any transfer to other metro lines. Many
stations often house improvised mini-markets.

Marshrutka

The *marshrutka* (shuttle bus) is yet another
example of the Ukrainian entrepreneurial spirit.
A number of popular city bus routes are
supplemented by these shuttle buses, which are

run by private companies. They are more reliable, run more often, and will stop by request in addition to their regular stops. You can flag down a *marshrutka* if there is a vacant seat and you are not standing under a "No Stopping" sign!

Trams, Trolleybuses, and Buses

There are several city tram networks in the cities of Kharkiv, Kyiv, Lviv, and Odesa. In Krivy Rig there is a speed tramline nearly seven and a half miles (12 km) long. Trolleybuses and buses are a cheap way to travel, but they can be crowded and stuffy in the summer. Tickets can be purchased in kiosks at the bus stops, and you have to punch the ticket inside the bus or trolleybus (or ask another passenger to do it for you). If the ticket is not punched, it is not valid.

DESTINATIONS

With its seaside resorts and spas, Ukraine was considered the health center of the former Soviet Union. After independence, Ukraine inherited more than 5,000 tourist establishments with capacity for 600,000 tourists at any one time.

Crimea

As Ukrainians say, the Russian tsars and nobility were no fools—they built their summer residences along the southern coast of Crimea. Sheltered from the northern winds by the mountains, this area has a dry, subtropical microclimate. On the same latitude as Venice, its summer temperatures are similar to those on the French and Spanish Mediterranean coasts. After the 1917 Revolution the Crimean palaces were turned into sanatoria and resort centers, with private parks, beaches, and health spas for the Soviet elite. Today these offer a full range of health and fitness treatments, ranging from massage, mud baths, saunas, and fitness training, to weight-loss programs and physiotherapy. The infrastructure, however, does not live up to the high prices.

Crimea is also known for its historical events. Sevastopol, a former Soviet military base that now plays host to the Russian Black Sea Fleet, has many

monuments to the Crimean War. It was where
Florence Nightingale started the nursing movement.

The Livadia Palace hosted the 1945 Yalta Con-
ference, attended by US president Franklin D.
Roosevelt, British prime minister Winston
Churchill, and the Soviet leader Joseph Stalin.

Odesa

Odesa was often called the "Pearl of the Black Sea."
Its sandy beaches, lively street life, and mixture of
architectural styles—from ornate French baroque
to Art Nouveau—give it a more Mediterranean
than Slavic feel. "Never, in any country, have so
many nationalities, with such opposing manners,
languages, clothes, religions, and customs, lived in
such a tiny area," wrote the Duc de Richelieu, the
French émigré Governor of Odesa, in a letter to
Tsar Alexander I in 1811.

Odesa remains the most cosmopolitan city in
Ukraine: over a hundred different nationalities
reside there, and non-Ukrainians make up more
than 45 percent of the population. Odesa retains
the spirit of a free port. It is an exciting place with
a laid-back attitude to life, and to authority. It has
a reputation for cheeky humor and, as we've seen,
celebrates "Yumorina," the festival of humor, on
April 1 every year.

Odesa used to be known as a Jewish city. At
the beginning of the twentieth century 33 percent

of its population spoke Yiddish. In the period 1970–90, the majority of Odesa's remaining Jews emigrated to Israel, the USA, and Russia, taking with them their irreverent Odesa humor. Ukrainians say that the inhabitants of Odesa never leave their city, but merely move it to another continent.

Western Ukraine

If you are a fan of active holidays, head to the Carpathian Mountains, which offer whitewater rafting, hiking, and trout fishing in the summer, and skiing in the winter. This area did not become part of the Soviet Ukraine until 1939, and the people here have a more entrepreneurial approach—once you get over the Soviet-style customs and bureaucracy!

The city of Lviv, the "capital" of Western Ukraine, is listed by Unesco as a world heritage city. It feels like a central European city: trams rattle along the cobbled streets; coffee shops on every corner advertise cakes "as Mother used to make"; many of the Renaissance-period buildings in the center have retained their original features. Even if you are a fluent Russian-speaker, English will be much better understood here.

WHERE TO STAY

High prices in Ukrainian hotels do not necessarily mean high quality. Apart from a few international-class hotels in Kyiv, Lviv, Donetsk, Odesa, and Yalta, hotel accommodation is not always up to international standards.

The three-star segment of the hotel industry is developing rapidly, and there is also a niche market of small, comfortable hotels. You can book a hotel in most of the large cities on the Internet (www.all-hotels.com.ua). Be warned that there are still many Soviet-style hotels with no stars.

The paucity of world-class hotels has created a large apartment-rental market. Most property companies have well-renovated, furnished and reasonably priced apartments for rent.

CURRENCY

The currency in Ukraine is called the hryvna (official sign UAH). One hryvna is worth 100 kopiyky. Banknotes are issued in 1, 2, 5, 10, 20, 50,

100, and 200 denominations. The modern name for the Ukrainian currency dates back to the eleventh century. In Kyivan Rus the aristocracy wore silver bars, used for payment, around their necks. They were called *gryvnas*, from the word *gryva*, which meant "neck." The modern Ukrainian currency replaced the Soviet ruble and came into circulation in 1996.

There are exchange booths in most Ukrainian cities where you can obtain hryvnas in exchange for Russian rubles, US dollars, and Euros; but make sure you count the money before you leave. If you have British pounds or Australian dollars, you need to go to a bank. You can also change money at hotels, railway stations, airports, and nightclubs, but the rates are less favorable to the visitor. There is normally no commission on currency exchange.

Credit Cards and ATMs

Though credit cards are widely accepted, Ukraine is still very much a cash economy. There are ATMs everywhere, and you can check with Visa or MasterCard online for a listing of all the ATMs in the cities you plan to visit. You may find them in big hotels, department stores, restaurants, or in the streets. Most dispense only Ukrainian currency, but in the largest cities (Kyiv, Odesa, Kharkiv, Donetsk) you can also draw US dollars. There is a fee for using ATMs, but it is considerably lower than that for using traveler's checks.

FINDING YOUR WAY

"Your tongue will lead you to Kyiv," says an old Ukrainian proverb. It goes back to the days when thousands of illiterate pilgrims, en route to the "holy bones" at Pechersk Lavra, could always find somebody to direct them to Kyiv. This proverb sums up the Ukrainian attitude to finding the way: you can always ask somebody.

Young Ukrainians speak reasonably good English. A taxi driver, even if he speaks only Ukrainian or Russian, will take you to an address if you show it to him written down, and will even escort you if the staircase is dark or you are unsure of the number of the block.

WHAT TO WEAR

The necessity of warm clothing in winter and practical shoes is worth a mention—it is very sad to see shivering foreigners battling the elements in thin coats. Ukrainian winters are supposed to be milder than Russian, but the temperature can go down to -13°F (-25°C). The Ukrainian name for February is *Luty*, which translates as "ferocious." Warm sheepskin jackets and coats, of different quality and various prices, are sold everywhere in Ukraine. Another miserable sight is a glamorously clad woman, teetering along the cobbled streets in the old parts of Kyiv or Lviv in high-heeled shoes. "If you can't afford good shoes, take a taxi," advises a Ukrainian joke.

It is worth making a reasonable effort when going out— Ukrainians judge a person by their appearance before getting to know them.

HEALTH

The health-care sector in Ukraine is overstretched and underfunded. Private medical insurance exists, but it is mandatory only for foreigners and for train passengers. If you are ill, you can go to a walk-in polyclinic, where you are treated for a small fee, or, in emergency, call an ambulance (03). You can also get a doctor's advice by phone (083), but the response will be in Ukrainian or Russian. Ukrainians often say that, "it is impossible to buy health," but you can buy good on-the-spot treatment if you call a private medical service, such as Medicom (055) or Boris (in Kyiv, 238 00 00). Or you can go to a foreign-owned private clinic, such as the American Medical Center.

The major health problems in Ukraine come from overindulgence in food and alcohol. Most pharmacies stock medications of various strengths for stomach upsets, digestive overload, and hangovers. You can call 067, a pharmacy information center, to check what medication is available in the pharmacy near you. If you are desperate, a private medical service (Medicom or Boris) can bring an intravenous detoxifying and rehydrating drip to your home. Ukrainians cope with the situation with a large number of "black" jokes.

The Right Illness

An American doctor asked his Ukrainian colleague, "Is it true that there are cases in your country where a patient has been treated for a particular disease, only to have the autopsy reveal a different cause of death?" "Absolutely not" replied the Ukrainian doctor, "All our patients die of the diseases we treat them for."

Vaccinations

Tetanus-diphtheria and hepatitis A vaccinations are recommended for all travelers, hepatitis B for those visiting for more than six months. Rabies vaccination is necessary for those who may have direct contact with animals. Typhoid vaccination is recommended for visitors who may be eating or drinking away from the major restaurants and hotels, and for travelers to Southern Ukraine.

Visitors should be aware that an estimated 350,000 people in Ukraine have AIDS or are HIV-positive, around 1.1 percent of the adult population. It is one of the legacies of the previous regime, which treated this problem with denial, ignorance, and fear. You should exercise normal precautions to avoid exposure to HIV/AIDS. There has been an increase in the number of cases of measles in Ukraine; the majority were in the territory of the Western Ukraine.

Radiation and Nuclear Safety
In 1986 the largest recorded accidental release of radioactive materials into the atmosphere occurred at Chornobyl. The highest areas of radioactive contamination of the ground came within around 19 miles (or around 30 km) of the Chornobyl nuclear station. The city of Kyiv was not as badly affected because of the favorable wind direction on the days following the accident. The Chornobyl nuclear power station was officially closed on December 15, 2000.

The Ukrainian government has a rigorous program of monitoring the fresh vegetables, fruit, and meat sold in local markets. Avoid wild berries, mushrooms, wildfowl, and game. Background levels of radiation are monitored regularly and to date have not exceeded the normally accepted levels.

TIPS ON SECURITY

- When traveling by train, lock your luggage. If you can afford it, take the whole compartment and lock yourself in.
- Beware of pickpockets in the street and when traveling on public transportation.
- Keep a photocopy of your passport and credit cards. Keep them in a safe place.
- Don't hail a private car late at night.
- Don't use an ATM on a dark street; go to a hotel or nightclub.
- Don't change money on the streets, or with an acquaintance. It is illegal, it can be dangerous, and you are likely to be cheated.
- Ukrainian girls are attractive, and flaunt their femininity. Watch out for tricks, though: there are occasional cases of drinks being spiked with drugs in the nightclubs. If a girl invites you to her apartment, think again—there may be a couple of toughs and/or a bogus taxi waiting for you outside.
- If you are really concerned for your safety, you can act like a movie star and hire a bodyguard for the duration of your stay— many former military, militia, or KGB officers now run private companies, offering a high level and quality of security services from personal protection to guarding premises.

SECURITY

After Independence Ukraine experienced a dramatic surge in crime. The real increase, according to the American National Institute of Justice, was not in violent crime but in theft, fraud, extortion, and economic crimes, such as bribery, counterfeiting, and drug dealing. Burglaries from apartments and vehicles represent the most significant threat to long-term residents. Although fewer cars are actually stolen, primarily because of the increased use of alarm systems and steering-wheel locks, break-ins and vandalism are increasing.

However, the levels of crime are low compared to those in most Western countries, and much lower than in Russia. The real numbers may be hidden by an inefficient system of crime recording and statistics; but a major contributor to crime levels is the spread of urbanization. The western regions of Ukraine are primarily rural and always had the lowest recorded crime levels. The highest levels are found in Kyiv, the Kharkiv region, Crimea, and particularly in the eastern industrial regions of Dnipropetrovsk, Donetsk, and Lugansk.

chapter eight

BUSINESS BRIEFING

THE BUSINESS ENVIRONMENT

Ukraine has many of the components necessary to become a major European economy. It has a developed industrial base, rich agricultural resources, and proximity to existing and untapped markets in Europe, Russia, and Asia. The majority of Soviet high-tech military plants were in Ukraine, and the country had, at the end of the Soviet era, a highly skilled engineering workforce and large manufacturing capacity.

Ukraine is one of the world's major sugar producers (sugar beet) and the fourth-largest steel producer. There is a developed road and railway infrastructure,

and an effective system of river ports and seaports. Crimea offers good opportunities for tourism. After independence in 1991, Ukraine had all the prerequisites for attracting a high level of foreign investment and becoming a major European player. However, in no other country in the region was there such a large gap between potential and actual economic performance. After contracting every year since independence, the Ukrainian economy reached a turning point with the introduction of macroeconomic reforms in 2000. In 2011 the full-year real GDP growth forecast was 4.8 percent.

CORRUPTION

Ukraine consistently ranks among the thirty-most corrupt countries in Transparency International's annual review. Corruption in penetrates all levels of business and administrative sectors. In a business survey conducted by the International Financial Corporation (IFC), only 18 percent of respondent companies indicated that they had not paid unofficial fees to obtain basic government services such as business permits, fire inspection reports, and so on. An active government campaign is bringing about a decrease in administrative corruption, but much remains to be done. As long as public servants' salaries remain low, illegal payments and bribes will persist.

Another severe threat to economic growth in Ukraine is the control of significant portions of the economy, particularly the mass media, energy, and heavy industries, by politically influential groups, referred to as "oligarchs." Fighting corruption and the investigation of high-profile criminal cases is the top priority of the new Ukrainian government.

The Shadow Economy

When Western analysts want to look at the poverty level in Ukraine, they look at the official income figures for the population. However, it is difficult for them to assess the scale of the "gray" (or, as Ukrainians call it, the "shadow") economy.

One only needs to look at the number of Mercedes cars and luxury boutiques in Kyiv and other cities to realize that official figures represent only part of the picture. Government policies aim to turn the shadow economy into legitimate economic activity.

FOREIGN INVESTMENT

The level of foreign direct investment is still alarmingly low. Most investors are deterred from doing business in Ukraine by the complexity of the tax and administrative regimes, concerns over political stability and corruption, and unclear legislation, in particular regarding property rights. As one European businessman put it, "The enchantment with Ukrainian opportunities is wiped away by the challenges of investment."

THE LEGAL SYSTEM

After independence Ukraine had to build a new judiciary and a completely new legal framework. The lack of experience available and the urgency of this huge challenge brought about an inconsistent and somewhat ambiguous legal system. At the beginning of 2000 Ukraine had a patchwork of laws, regulations, decrees, and resolutions that often contradicted each other. One result is that, while law-abiding foreign businessmen spend a fortune on consultants and lawyers, the middle level of ministerial bureaucrats and customs and tax officials have a field day ruling on such contradictions. "The laws are for the poor . . . ," "Those who are stronger and smarter will always find their way around them," are typical Ukrainian clichés. However, the introduction of significant legal reforms and the passing of the Land, Customs, Civil, and Commercial Codes show that Ukraine is establishing a new code of law consistent with EU practice. Passing new legislation is only a first step. There is a long way to go to achieve transparency and enforcement.

THE BUSINESS CULTURE
Soviet Legacy and European Aspirations

The Ukrainian business culture is a unique blend
of the Soviet past and new European aspirations.
The Soviet legacy manifests itself in a reluctance
to make decisions (decisions were usually made
"above you"), in long-term centralist planning
(namely, the Soviet five-year plans), and in a lack
of understanding of market forces and market
needs. In the former USSR, forecasting and
ordering were always implemented through the
centralized planning committees in Moscow.
However, twenty years of independence have led
to a well-traveled, progressive-minded, English-
speaking younger generation. These are the people
to employ as agents and managers in your local
offices. They will understand the ins and outs of
the complex bureaucracy; they will find out the
implications of new or amended legislation; and
they will use the right business contacts.

Attitude Toward Authority

"You are nothing without a piece of paper," went a
popular Soviet saying. Businessmen often cannot
fully function without getting a stamp of approval,
in fact, a decision, from the authorities. Fear of the
Soviet authorities has been gradually replaced by
mistrust and disapproval of the government of the
day. Ukrainians have seen so many government

changes over the last twenty years that they have become suspicious of any government institution.

Suspicion of the government has led to the development of a networking system, where business is conducted on the level of personal trust rather than professional qualities. Relations and close friends often become business partners.

It's All Personal

Strong family ties and friendships have been a survival mechanism for centuries in Ukraine, be it in farming, when families pooled resources, or in times of hardship and crisis. Friendship and connections make all the difference between success and failure. A network of personal contacts is the most valued asset in getting something done. Ukrainians expect friendship to extend to business. They will be fiercely loyal and trusting, and will work hard for those they are bonded to.

Middlemen

Businessmen coming to Ukraine for the first time need somebody to lead them through the bureaucratic and regulatory maze. There are many companies, expatriate and Ukrainian, ranging from local law firms to customs and import rules specialists, that will offer help as consultants. Don't necessarily reject the approaches, but be careful whom you choose. Ukrainians are quicker on promises than delivery. Also, if someone, even introduced by a friend, confidently promises, "Yes, I can do it," they will be expecting generous "thanks" in advance. Try to avoid this situation.

Always check the track record and solvency of any company you may be doing business with. Your embassy in Kyiv will have a commercial section that may be able to advise. Other sources of information are the local chambers of commerce.

Work Ethic

Ukraine's northern neighbors call it "Ukrainian greed," Europeans call it "work motivation," but the bottom line is the same: Ukrainians are responsible and hardworking. In the former USSR they were known for being prepared to work in the hardest and harshest conditions to give their families a better standard of living. Most of the Siberian oil rigs, for example, were (and many still are) manned by Ukrainian engineers. The trend continued after the fall of the USSR. As the economy collapsed in the 1990s around 1.5 million Ukrainians (according to official figures, although unofficial estimates are much higher) went to work abroad in hospitals, construction, catering, and industry.

In Portugal, for example, the government decided to issue work permits for Ukrainian workers, despite the EU recommendation to reduce the inflow of migrant workers into the EU. Urbano Constanca de Souza, a senior adviser on immigration at the Ministry of Home Affairs in Lisbon, stated that, "the people of Ukraine are often highly skilled, they are motivated to work, and neither complain nor cause problems. They are able to pick up the language quickly, and it is not unusual to find a Ukrainian who speaks better Portuguese after six months than someone from Angola who has been here for twenty years."

Don't Watch the Clock

"The farmers work hard, and then watch the plants grow"; "Soviet workers have got all the time in the world for a smoking break as the state will pay their salaries anyway." Whichever way you look at it, you need to understand the Ukrainian approach to time. It is incomprehensible to the punctual British or the organized Americans— why does somebody call to say that he is running ten minutes late, and then turn up an hour late? Why is a meeting at a ministry, arranged months in advance, delayed for two hours?

Ukrainians have a more relaxed approach to time. In everyday conversations you are likely to hear, "Come around seven," or "Let's meet at about five." If somebody calls to say that they will be ten minutes late, you'll have time to read the newspaper.

Promises to Deliver

"You led me on and let me down," is the refrain of the most popular Ukrainian folk song, in which a girl promises to meet a boy on Monday, Tuesday, Wednesday . . . all through the week—and never turns up. Ukrainians often go back on their word, forget to return calls and messages, or simply don't deliver. Most frequently it will be done without any malicious intent, and no hard feelings are expected. The Ukrainian nonconfrontational approach is, "It is easier to avoid saying "no," so that the person will not be upset, and then "forget" to do it afterward." How to deal with it? Just be cool and patient. If somebody confidently promises to deliver something at the first meeting, don't assume that it will be done.

"Initiative Is There To Be Punished"

Rather than act with authority and make business decisions, managers often opt to take the frustrating "let's urgently wait and see" attitude. Throughout its history Ukraine was run as a part of a larger empire. People learned to be reactive, not proactive, in their approach to life. In the twentieth century, during the Stalinist purges, to shift the blame or responsibility could often mean personal survival. For decades the Soviet system followed the principle, "Initiative is there to be punished."

As a result, managers of the older generation, who have had firsthand experience of the Soviet economic machine, are often reluctant to take risks and make decisions. The new, emerging management style in Ukraine is to have a more international approach to business, interested in innovation and the introduction of international corporate practices. In essence, a "yes" from a sixty-year-old Ukrainian director is very different from a "yes" from a thirty-year-old one.

Hierarchies

It is often forgotten, or overlooked, that Ukraine made a jump from a totalitarian regime to a democracy in two decades. Other countries have been developing their democracies for centuries. The Communist Party hierarchy neither held their leaders to account nor consulted with the people. Orders from the top were for execution, not for questioning. One of the major problems of Ukrainian business culture stems from this acceptance of hierarchical control. Ukrainian managers find the concept of delegating responsibility quite challenging. Many are accustomed to running a tight ship, in full control from the top. A common attitude is, "As it is my signature on the document, it is my responsibility and my decision only." Therefore, there is still a gap between the "leader," who assigns tasks and gives orders, and the executor, who implements those tasks without questioning them. An illustration of this is provided by the Ukrainian graduate who took a job in a top American bank, and started his first working day with the question, "Who is going to tell me what to do?"

Team Spirit

Surprisingly for a post-Communist country, team spirit at work is extremely rare. Its absence can be explained partly by past disillusionment with unattainable Communist "common goals," and partly by the uncertainties of the transitional economy. "Will the company be there tomorrow?" "What should I do to keep my job?" These issues are more important to employees than a corporate vision or goals.

Personal survival is often more important to the individual than the company's growth. "If you want to save your job, don't share your ideas with anybody," was the recent advice given in a national women's magazine. And, of course, there is the underlying Soviet mentality of "Why should I exert myself? It's not my company." Moreover, as new corporate ethics develop in Ukraine, it is difficult to engage everyone, as many companies still do not have clear corporate goals. If they exist, they may be in the minds of top management only!

Praise Is Rare

Praise is rare in Ukrainian organizations. Doing a good job is expected and taken for granted. When an employee is summoned by the manager, the expectation is admonishment or dismissal, certainly not praise! The Soviet principle, "All workers should be equally professional; we should punish those who are holding us back," is thoroughly ingrained.

Too Good to be True!
The Ukrainian sales manager of a retail company in Kyiv was praised on her monthly results by a newly appointed Dutch sales director. After the meeting she turned to her Ukrainian colleague in bewilderment: "Why did Peter say, 'Well done, Irina!'—do you think he was being sarcastic?"

WOMEN IN BUSINESS
The financial director (or equivalent) holds one of the most respected positions in any Ukrainian company or organization. He or she is the person who pays the salaries, talks to the tax inspectors, develops the budget, and prepares the annual report. Ukrainians often joke that only a woman can cope with such multitasking. Traditionally, the chief accountants and financial directors of the majority of Ukrainian companies have indeed been women. Teachers, pediatricians, and family doctors are also traditionally female professions in Ukraine.

Although women constitute some 52 percent of university graduates, only 20 percent of middle managers and 5.8 percent of top managers are women. There is a similar picture in politics: there are very few women in the leadership of political parties, and male MPs far outnumber female ones in Parliament. Ukraine, sadly, ranks 106th out of 134 countries when it comes to women's representation in bodies of power.

Nataliya Rudnichenko, a Ukrainian journalist, said, "Society's attitude is that women in Ukraine must always remember that they are only 'sergeants' and men hold the senior ranks. Women must always remember where they belong, and must never aspire to become generals."

CONDUCTING A MEETING

Wear a conservative suit. A smart, businesslike appearance is important, and the make of your watch and the color of your tie will be noticed.

Be prepared for meetings to start late, or to be canceled at the last minute. Be ready for the waiting game, when a secretary will repeatedly ask you to call again "within an hour," or inform you for the fifth time that her boss will be back "any minute now." It is said that it is better to plan a meeting for the morning, as it will give you more time to wait. You, however, are expected to be punctual. Waiting is the norm in Ukraine, so don't show your frustration at the meeting when it finally takes place. It will not be appreciated.

When your counterpart enters the room, shake hands, introduce yourself, and offer your business card. If several people join a meeting, you may have to stop and engage in a full round of handshaking.

Business cards are essential. Recognition of your position in your company's hierarchy is important. The title "Senior Vice President" on a card will carry more weight than "Sales Executive" or "Project Manager." See yourself through the eyes of your customer—your title is the key both to your level of access and to how seriously you are taken. It is a good idea to have the reverse of your business cards printed in Ukrainian.

It might be stating the obvious, but it is crucial to have a good interpreter. Foreign companies often choose their Russian-speaking specialists to send to Ukraine. This can offend their counterparts, especially in the Western part of the country.

A Ukrainian business leader's office is his castle. It is a place not only to talk, but often also to entertain, and a secretary may pour tea or vodka. Also it is normal to find bottles of mineral water or soft drinks on the table in front of you, complete with bottle opener. Feel free to open a bottle and pour yourself a drink if you are thirsty.

NEGOTIATION

Business negotiations can be quite long-winded. Ukrainians will start the dialogue with a long "warm-up" session about the journey, the family, or that evening's proposed entertainment. Don't get impatient; any attempt to rush straight into business is considered rude. The beginning of the meeting is a time for evaluating the person one is dealing with.

While Western negotiators prefer a sequential approach and tackle every issue separately, Ukrainians tend to come to an understanding on the "global picture" first, before getting into the details of a proposition or contract. Sometimes a Ukrainian host may say, to start the negotiations, "Well, that's how we see it. And what is your proposal?" The Westerner is not always prepared for such a direct and abrupt beginning. Be very careful with your answer, as this initial statement will be considered the backbone of your proposal. A long, detailed discussion does not necessarily lead to a decision to proceed to contract.

Ukrainians consider early compromise to be a sign of weakness and will give minimal or no concessions. Recent research by the Institute of Sociology in Kyiv showed that Ukrainians say the word "no" nine times more often in negotiation than their Western counterparts . So be prepared for a curt "No!" to be the first response to your proposal. Though used frequently, it does not necessarily negate a discussion or the suggestion at hand. Try to approach the matter in a different way. Continue to talk about details, deliveries, and so on. Leave the price until last, even when asked, and do not give a "ballpark" figure, because your counterparts will take this as your firm price. Save any final price concession for the last meeting, even up to half an hour before you leave for the airport. You will be respected for tenacity and professionalism.

The Ukrainian approach to negotiation can be emotional and direct, with "no" as the best-case scenario, and raised voices and walking out as the worst case. History records the notorious incident at the UN Security Council session in New York in the 1960s, when the then Soviet leader, Nikita Khrushchev—a Ukrainian—shouted, "We will show you!" and banged his shoe on the table.

THE WRITTEN WORD

If you have discussed the entire plan with your counterparts and agreed upon every possible combination of events that could occur, you may be asked to sign a "Protocol of Intent." This is effectively a memorandum of the meeting, which is considered by Ukrainians as the first landmark on the long route to a business relationship and a contract. The "Protocol of Intent" is a "binding in principle" document, signed by both parties. It is generally not enforceable by law. It usually comprises a summary of the points of agreement from a meeting or series of meetings and can be the springboard to a contract. The Ukrainian side will recall the protocol at the next meeting, so don't throw it away!

Keep contracts simple, straightforward, and wherever possible conforming to Ukrainian legal standards. It is often a good idea to take the initiative by putting your contract proposal on the table first. In final negotiations, especially for high-value or complex contracts, it is always advisable to have your company's legal representative at the table. This saves time and irons out unforeseen legal consequences during the contract negotiations. However, beware: the more complex you make your contracts, the easier it will be for someone to find a way to break them. A contract will generally be translated into the Ukrainian language, and both copies signed. In addition your "company stamp" will be required as the official confirmation of your signature, and it is therefore advisable to bring with you a self-inking rubber company seal.

Finally, however tiring the day (or, more likely, the week) of negotiations has been, don't refuse an invitation to dinner. As Ukrainians love to entertain, toasting at the dinner table is just as important as the work achieved in the morning's negotiations, if not more so. It is a part of building trust and loyalty.

MANAGING DISAGREEMENT

Should a contract give rise to disagreement, the dispute can be lengthy and costly. Your best bet is to find a Ukrainian lawyer or a Western firm established in Ukraine, as the laws change often. Sometimes seemingly irrational decisions by your Ukrainian partners may be influenced by a change in a tax law or new export rules. Try to clarify the situation with them amicably at first. The better your personal relationship with your partners, the easier it will be to reach a compromise.

CONCLUSION

The Ukrainian business scene is a blend of the Soviet legacy and today's complex tax and regulatory structures, finessed with local entrepreneurial spirit. Despite these challenges, business in Ukraine does go on and in many cases presents unprecedented opportunities. If you understand the local customs and are open, direct, and professional, you will be respected in Ukraine. Doing business here is not always easy, but is guaranteed to be exciting, if not a little frustrating at times. Socializing and friendliness outside the office will more than compensate for the setbacks.

chapter nine

COMMUNICATING

THE LANGUAGE ISSUE

According to data from the
All-Ukrainian census of 2001,
67.5 percent of the population of
Ukraine regarded Ukrainian as
their native tongue, and
52 percent of the population
admitted that they used more Russian
in everyday life. Ukraine has the highest number
of nonnative Russian speakers after Russia.

"Russification" started in Ukraine in 1720 with
the decree of Peter the Great banning the printing
and publication of books in Ukrainian. The policy
of the Tsarist empire was followed by Soviet Russia
with a number of decrees. In 1983, for example,
the Russian language was given priority status in
Ukrainian schools, with teachers of Russian being
better paid. Being fluent in Russian was a
precondition of a successful career and a higher
social status in Soviet times.

Since independence in 1991 the Ukrainian
language has gained the status of official national

language. About 80 percent of secondary education is now conducted in Ukrainian. The language problem remains, however, and is so important that in the 2010 presidential elections one of the candidates, Viktor Yanukovych, as part of his election campaign, promised to give the Russian language the status of second official language in Ukraine.

You will find it useful to learn the Ukrainian alphabet before your visit. It is based on the Cyrillic alphabet and is similar to Russian, but several letters are different. At least you won't have to go hungry when you see the word РЕСТОРАН on every corner—it is pronounced "restaurant!" If the prospect is too daunting, don't despair. Most of the younger generation speaks English, with various degrees of fluency.

FORMAL AND INFORMAL ADDRESS

There are two forms of address in Ukrainian: the polite second person (and plural) *vy* and the familiar second person (and singular) *ty*. It is considered rude to use the familiar form when you meet someone for the first time, unless they are very young. Always use the polite form until you are invited to use the familiar one. The invitation to do so is a sign that your friendship with the native speaker has reached a warmer, more intimate level.

The polite form *vy* is joined by the name and patronymic (the fathers' name plus a suffix, *ivna/yivna* for a female, and *ovych* for a man). For example, Mariya Mykolayivna means "Maria, daughter of Mykola"; Serhiy Olexandrovych is "Serhiy, son of Olexandr." Addressing people by their first name, especially in an official business situation, is considered rude.

The form of address is even more confusing to the foreigner, as there is no direct equivalent in Ukraine of Mr., Mrs., and Miss. The previously convenient unisex Communist form of address *tovarysh* (comrade) is now obsolete. The restored prerevolutionary forms of address *Pane* (Mr.) and *Pani* (Mrs./Miss), though used, are not yet commonly accepted. People use amusing ways of addressing a stranger in a public place. A middle-aged woman might be addressed as "Girl," to her delight, and a man as "Man in the gray hat," or "Man with the dog."

FACE-TO-FACE
Ukrainians love to talk. Simply asking, "How are you?" can interrupt your day for hours, as the other person will feel obliged to involve you in a range of topics from the minor ailments of her mother-in-law to her plans for the summer break.

But if you, in your turn, answer, "Fine, thank you," and carry on, you will be treated with suspicion or might even offend your friend, as such curt behavior will be considered rude.

"It's Good to Talk"

Two Ukrainian women who had shared a prison cell for three years were set free. They walked through the prison gates, and two hours later they were still standing talking outside the gates. "Why are you still here?" inquired a curious prison guard, "You are free to go." "We know," answered one, "We just need to finish our chat."

The loquacious nature of Ukrainians is most evident in their celebratory toasts and speeches. "He is a real politician," Ukrainians might say about a public speaker who would talk for hours but say nothing new or enlightening. The ability to talk for a long time about something that could be expressed concisely is a legacy of the Soviet education system, which encouraged long essays and many words to articulate a simple thought.

The structure of the Ukrainian language is direct, and may seem abrupt to foreigners, but this is not intentional. Ukrainian forms of politeness are much simpler than English, and as a result, Ukrainians can sound brusque to English ears.

Lost in Translation

A young lawyer from the Kyiv office of an international law firm was sent to the head office in London for three months. Her English was quite fluent. She was modest and diligent, and was very surprised, at the end of her time there, that her appraisal labeled her as "lacking politeness to the point of being rude and almost arrogant." She had simply been translating perfectly polite Ukrainian patterns of speech into English; but she rarely said "please" and "thank you," and her requests sounded like orders.

BODY LANGUAGE AND PERSONAL SPACE

Years of communal living led to the closing up of personal space during conversations. People will seem to be standing threateningly close to you. They may pat your shoulder and, if they know you well, give you a hug. Women often walk arm in arm. Don't take it personally if you are jostled in the bus, or if somebody pushes to the head of a line. This habit stems from the Soviet era, when people had to storm a bus or train to get to work or push ahead to buy winter fruit for a child.

> ### *GESTURES*
> - Don't point with your index finger; this is considered uncultured.
> - Don't put your thumb between your first two fingers—this is a very rude gesture. It's called *doolya*, and means "You are not getting it!" and, in fact, it has been used as a symbol of defiance against Ukraine's invaders and oppressors for centuries.
> - Don't keep your hands in your pockets when you talk to your superior or an elderly person—it looks disrespectful.
> - On a positive note, you can always give the "thumbs up" sign to show your approval.

THE MEDIA

Today young people tend to get their news from the Internet, but for most older people in Ukraine the main source of information is still the press.

The key papers are *Zerkalo Nedeli* (a political weekly with English-language pages), *Den* (daily, with English-language pages), *Kyiv Post* (the most objective English-language daily in Ukraine), and *Ukrayinska Pravda* (online news, with English-language pages). While most newspaper publishers are private—only a small percentage are state-owned—this does not prevent the authorities from trying to influence what is published. In recent years the situation for the opposition media has become difficult. The authorities have closed down several opposition papers and control, directly or indirectly, almost all TV channels. Even so, the press in Ukraine is freer than it is in neighboring Russia.

Radio

Radio has a smaller audience than television. Around 72 percent of Ukrainians listen to the radio occasionally; 46 percent listen to it every day. The most popular broadcaster is the cable radio service run by the state-owned National Radio Company of Ukraine, thanks to the extensive cable radio network developed in Soviet times.

SERVICES
Telephone

Usually, telephone calls within the city area are free (except for those made through some phone companies), so conversations do not need to be short. Be prepared for long ones!

Callers don't always introduce themselves. "Ask him to call me," or "Is Irina there?" are classic examples of the telephone style. Ukrainians don't like talking to an answering machine. "A machine does not replace a human voice," they feel, so often they don't leave or respond to messages.

DIALING CODES

The international phone code for Ukraine is 38.

To call Ukraine from elsewhere:

Dial the international access code in your country, then dial: 38 (international code for Ukraine) + city code + subscriber's number.

For example, to call Odesa 123 456 from the USA, dial: 011 38 0482 123 456. (011 is the international access code from the U.S.A.; 38 is Ukraine's international code; 0482 is Odesa's city code.)

To make a city-to-city call:

Wait for the dial tone, dial 8 (intercity access code), wait for the new dial tone, then dial the area code and the subscriber's number.

To call abroad from Ukraine:

Wait for the dial tone, dial 8 (intercity access code), wait for the new dial tone, then dial 10 (international access code) + country code + area code (if required) + subscriber's number.

Ukraine's outdated fixed-line network is gradually being upgraded and replaced by new digital exchanges, especially in the cities. However, the quality of the connection can vary from excellent in Kyiv to very poor in a small town or village. Ukrtelecom, the state-owned telecom giant, has 80 percent of the domestic market in the number of subscribers. The majority of private local operators are niche players. The protracted and controversial privatization of Ukrtelecom has had a negative impact on the modernization of the fixed line networks and services.

All calls are charged by the minute. Hotels tend to charge two to three times more than the standard phone company charge. Because of the high rates of international calls, IP-telephone cards have become increasingly popular. Though the connection quality is worse, IP charges are three to four times lower. Cards can be bought in shops and post offices, and at newsstands.

Cell Phones

The cell phone market, particularly the prepaid segment, has grown spectacularly in the last few years, and in Kyiv land lines are being displaced by the wide choice of GSM or CDMA operators. Cell phones also have great cachet as status symbols.

All incoming calls are free. Visitors can buy a cell phone with a SIM card, or simply put the SIM card (prepaid package) into their own phone (provided it supports such standards as GSM 900 or GSM 1800), and use it for both domestic and international calls. Prepaid packages are provided by all

Ukrainian cell phone operators and can be bought in shops selling cell phones or at stands selling prepaid cards.

Ukrainian cell phone users love text messaging. The Internet is improving across the country, and roaming is available from all operators.

Mail

Ukraine's mail services began in 1669 with the establishment of a postal yard with some forty horses. Today Ukrposhta, the national postal operator, has a network of 15,000 post offices throughout the country. Though the horses are long gone, the services are still painfully slow, albeit inexpensive. Delivery within Ukraine takes three to seven days, while mail to or from abroad takes seven to fourteen days.

Couriers provide faster and more effective delivery services. The majority of international couriers have offices in Ukraine. When sending a parcel to Ukraine it is worthwhile considering that valuables and CDs are subject to customs clearance, and this can cause additional delays and expense. Food, live plants, and animals are prohibited items, unless the recipient has special permission from the appropriate Ukrainian government authorities.

The Internet

The Internet is developing rapidly in Ukraine. A large number of Internet cafés and clubs provide free Wi-Fi access. Unlike the USA and Western Europe, the Ukrainian market for Internet services depends more on the availability of the telecom infrastructure and PCs than on the demand for ISP services. It is the low level of PC ownership in Ukraine that restricts the growth of Internet use.

CONCLUSION

Ukraine, at the crossroads of East and West, is eager to be seen as European, but needs to work hard to counter its reputation as an autocratic and politically unstable state. It also needs to establish relations with Russia on equal terms, and to find a clearer voice for its European aspirations.

What always strikes the visitor is the heady mix of ancient history and youthful energy, the resilience of the Ukrainian people and their generosity of spirit. For the twentieth anniversary of its independence, Ukraine received quite a present—hosting the key matches of Euro 2012. Now it has a game of its own: to show the world that the country at the crossroads is a serious player.

Further Reading

Dolot, Miron. *Execution by Hunger: The Hidden Holocaust.* New York: W.W. Norton & Company Ltd, 1987.

Dougan, Andy. *Dynamo.* London: Fourth Estate, 2002.

Hodges, Linda, and George Chumak. *Language and Travel Guide to Ukraine.* New York: Hippocrene Books, Inc., 2000.

Reid, Anna. *Borderland: A Journey Through the History of the Ukraine.* London: Weidenfeld & Nicolson, 2003.

Smith, Tim (Photographer), Rob Perks, and Graham Smith. *Ukraine's Forbidden History.* Stockport: Dewi Lewis Publishing, 1998.

Wilson, Andrew. *The Ukrainians: Unexpected Nation.* Yale: Yale Nota Bene, 2002.

Zahny, Bohdan. *The Best of Ukrainian Cuisine* New York: Hippocrene Books, Inc., 1998.

Appendix 1: The Ukrainian Alphabet

Ukrainian Alphabet	English Sound	Pronunciation Example
А а	ah	as in arm
Б б	b	as in box
В в	v	as in victory
Г г	g	as in ghost
Д д	d	as in day
Е е	eh	as in merry
Є є	ye	as in yellow
Ж ж	zh	as in pleasure
З з	z	as in zoo
И и	i	as in rink
І і	ee	as in see
Ї ї	yi	as in yield
Й й	y	as in yours
К к	k	as in kid
Л л	l	as in look
М м	m	as in man
Н н	n	as in night
О о	o	as in cot
П п	p	as in pot
Р р	r	as in red (rolled, as in Scots)
С с	s	as in sun
Т т	t	as in time
У у	oo	as in spoon
Ф ф	f	as in free
Х х	ch	as in the Scottish "loch"
Ц ц	ts	as in hats
Ч ч	ch	as in church
Ш ш	sh	as in she
Щ щ	shch	as in borshch
Ь ь		(indicates softness of consonants)
Ю ю	yoo	as in you
Я я	yah	as in yahoo

Appendix 2: Some Basic Words and Phrases

The stress falls on the syllables in **bold**.

Hello   *dobry **dehn***
Please   bood' ***las**-kah*
Thank you   ***dyah**-koo-yooh*
Yes   *tak*
No   *ni*
I'm sorry   ***vy**bachte*
Good-bye   *do po**ba**chennya*
I can't speak Ukrainian   *ya ne ho**vo**-ryoo oo-kra-**yin**-skoyoo*
Do you speak English?   *vy ho**vo**ryte anhleeyskoyu?*
I don't understand   *ya ne ro zoo –**mee** yu!*
I'm lost   *ya zahoo-**byv**sya*
How much is a ticket to __?   ***skeelky** **kosh**tuye **kvytok** do__*
How do I get to __?   *yak mojna dis**ta**tysya do*
. . . the train station?   *zali**znych**noyi **stan**tsiyi*
. . . the airport?   *ae**ro**portu*
. . . downtown?   ***tsen**tra mista*
A beer/two beers, please   *pyvo/ dva pyva, bood **las**-kah*
Can I look at the menu, please?   ***mozh**nah me**nyoo**,bood-**las**kah?*
I would like to   *ya b hotiv* (masc.)
                                       ya b hotila (fem.)

Taxi!   *taksi!*
Take me to _____, please.   *vidve**zit** 'mene____, bud **las**kah*
How much does it cost to get to __?   *skilky **kosh**tuye pro**yizd** do__?*
Left   *na**li**vo*
Right   *na**pra**vo*
Straight ahead   *vpe**red***

Common Signs

Open   **Відчинено**
Closed   **Зачинено**
Entrance   **Вхід**
Exit   **Вихід**
Push   **Від себе**
Pull   **До себе**
Toilet   **Туалет**

Index

Acknowledgments

This book is dedicated to my … self, than Fedia Sherebenko … prominent

… Natalia
… day life and
… Burbidge-
… ript; and